Brown Boy

Brown Boy

OMER AZIZ

A Memoir

SCRIBNER

LONDON NEW YORK SYDNEY TORONTO NEW DELHI

First published in the United States by Scribner,
an imprint of Simon & Schuster Inc., 2022

First published in Great Britain by Scribner,
an imprint of Simon & Schuster UK Ltd, 2022

SCRIBNER and design are registered trademarks of The Gale Group, Inc.,
used under licence by Simon & Schuster Inc.

1 3 5 7 9 10 8 6 4 2

Simon & Schuster UK Ltd
1st Floor
222 Gray's Inn Road
London WC1X 8HB

Simon & Schuster Australia, Sydney
Simon & Schuster India, New Delhi

www.simonandschuster.co.uk
www.simonandschuster.com.au
www.simonandschuster.co.in

A CIP catalogue record for this book
is available from the British Library

Hardback ISBN: 978-1-4711-9033-9
Trade paperback ISBN: 978-1-4711-9034-6
eBook ISBN: 978-1-4711-9035-3
Audio ISBN: 978-1-3985-1301-3

Printed and Bound in the UK using 100% Renewable
Electricity at CPI Group (UK) Ltd

For my teachers

And the mind that has conceived a plan of living must never lose sight of the chaos against which that pattern was conceived. That goes for societies as well as individuals.

—Ralph Ellison, *Invisible Man*

Thou shalt neither vex a stranger, nor oppress him: for ye were strangers in the land of Egypt.

—Exodus 22:21

Prologue

(2016)

The door closed in a brightly lit office. A soldier in a green uniform stood at the side. The interrogation chamber was about to swallow another body.

I sat in a chair, quiet and afraid. My eyes were fixed on the ground that now felt like quicksand. In America, I would have known what to say and do. But I was no longer in America. I was in Israel.

An hour passed, then another. The room was quiet, and except for the rush of thoughts, I was still. It was like those days of youth when I sat in the mosque and tried to talk to God. Now I was older and knew that God didn't talk to people in interrogation rooms.

A young soldier, boyish and hesitant, watched from the doorway. He must have been eighteen, nineteen tops. Our skin tones and facial features were similar. He reminded me of my boyhood friends back in Toronto, and in an amusing sort of way, resembled my younger self: in an alternative universe, our positions might have been reversed.

Despite being innocent of any wrongdoing, I could not understand why I still felt guilty.

A short, bald man entered the room. He had a folder under his arm, the reserved demeanor of a man in control.

"I am Max," he said. He rolled up his sleeves, sat across from me, and stared.

"Where are you from?" he asked.

"Canada," I said. "But I study in America."

"Omer . . ." he said. "This is a Hebrew name. You are Jewish?"

"No," I said, almost as an apology.

"Where is your family from?"

"Pakistan," I said.

Max's eyebrows went up. He ripped off a piece of paper and slid it toward me. "Write here your father's name. Write your father's birthplace. Write your grandfather's name, grandfather's birthplace, and all the relatives you have in Pakistan, Canada, and America."

I stared at the blank paper. I had been to Pakistan only once, when I was a boy, and had no memories of the country. I wasn't even sure how many relatives I had there anymore. My link to that nation existed through my parents and the culture I carried with me, a product of history, migration, and colonization. Pakistan was an imaginary homeland.

My hands grew sweaty. I rubbed them against my jeans. In an instant, I could see the chasm between the idea I had of myself—law student, reader, writer—and the perceptions forming in Max's eyes.

I answered his questions. I wrote my grandfather's birthplace as "British India," but I did not know anything else. I did not even know my own history.

Over the next four hours, Max asked me every possible question about my life. He asked if I practiced Islam, asked why I had come to his country, asked about my parents and friends. It was not lost on me that Max's own ancestors might have been put in ghettos, that he might have also been a descendant of the colonized.

Here was the truth: I was not a terrorist but a tourist, in my second year at Yale Law School, visiting the Holy Land with my peers so that we future lawyers could understand Israel and Palestine. In one way, this interrogation room was familiar, since I had been questioned all my life about my identity and religion. I could have been at any border crossing in the West, no longer an individual but viewed as part of the Brown mass gathering at the barbed-wire fences of our democracies. Straight-haired, lightly bearded with brown skin, I had the sort of face you might have seen on the television screen, every day and night, for over twenty years.

Now I regretted my decision to come on this trip, the only Brown person to join, the only person to be interrogated. Despite being warned of this possibility, I decided to go anyway because of the ideas I held in my heart: that one must live "as if" the trials of race and belonging did not exist, rising above prejudices and stereotypes, acting so free that one's very presence was an assault on the systems of injustice. Growing up after 9/11, I had found it impossible to craft a coherent identity when the whole world seemed to be losing its mind. My parents, immigrants and Muslims, were conflicted about how I should approach the world: to assimilate entirely or hold fast to my roots. I was torn within myself, trying to be two people at once, part of two cultures, finding acceptance in neither. So I boomeranged between invisibility and presence, between misperception and clarified reality, always trying to blend in, chameleon-like, with my environment. I had become a hyphenated man; no, I *was* the hyphen.

Even as the interrogator's pen clicked and the clock ticked, another question formed in my mind: What kind of dream had I been pursuing all these years, trying to educate myself out of my own skin, reading every book I could get my hands on, separating myself from my past, that in a single instant this stranger could put me right back into the box from which I sprang? Did I seriously think that I could escape from my tribe, liberate myself from the ordeals of Brown people, *my* people? How could I be so naive to believe that by "earning" the right badges and degrees, I might convince the inquisitors of the West that I was a worthy human being? I had unconsciously come to believe a lie.

At the end of a long four hours, the very identity—the mask—that I had carefully cultivated was peeled off like a false skin, leaving only the naked face underneath.

Eventually, I was free to go. "Let us know if you make any friends while you're in town," Max said. I did not answer him.

I got into a taxi with a white American friend, who asked how it went. I could not bring myself to speak, but I was burning inside.

We drove toward Jerusalem. The rolling hills passed us by, one of those beautiful Levantine evenings that seemed to portend the beginning and the end of worlds. And against this beautiful backdrop, I could feel the old fear and anger stirring in my chest, emotions I had taught myself to keep rigidly caged. I had learned the hard way that while the unexamined life might be more blissful, the examined life—from the eyes of a Brown boy—is a long trial: a crucible, or a crusade, set at the border between East and West.

Three days later, I awoke early in the morning and walked with my friends to the Dome of the Rock. I had already worn a yarmulke and prayed at the Western Wall, had seen pilgrims falling to their knees in the Church of the Holy Sepulchre, had watched as countless soldiers with machine guns watched me. I wanted to visit the Haram al-Sharif, or Dome of the Rock, the third holiest site in Islam, where it was believed that the Prophet Muhammad had flown to the heavens. I wanted to bring a Qur'an home for my mother.

As I walked, I was cognizant of my every move. I felt the alienation like rocks under my skin, an outsider, in conquered territory, among dueling histories and tragedies. I thought that after my treatment by the interrogators I would be welcomed in the holy mosque the minute I stepped inside and recited the ritual greeting of *As-salamu alaykum*. Peace be upon you.

I went through multiple checkpoints in the Old City and soon arrived at the stone steps. The mosque was brilliant, palatial, the golden dome glinting in the sunlight, the blue calligraphy harkening to centuries past.

An old man, the mosque's guardian, was standing outside the door and watching me and my friends. He had a tasbih in his hands and a gray beard that went to his chest. I had spent many years as a boy attending a madrassa in Toronto, so I knew what to say and how to carry myself. I told my friends I was going inside—technically, only Muslims were allowed to enter the old mosque, one of the few privileges I thought was mine.

5

The old man disappeared inside the masjid. I paused, considered waiting until he was back so he did not think that a Western traveler he had just seen taking photographs was trying to sneak into this place of worship. Once again, I doubted my place in my community, felt the need to adjust and wait, lest I be seen as an intruder. Then I decided, not for the last time, to act "as if" I belonged.

I walked slowly, the seconds stretching out with each step I took. Only when I crossed the threshold to the mosque did the old man see me.

He grabbed my shoulders and pushed me outside the door. My friends watched in horror as several guards rushed over to me.

"Who are you?" the old man shouted.

I stumbled over my words.

"Where are you from?"

I told him.

"You are a *kaafir*," he said, a nonbeliever.

He said something in Arabic to the security guards around me. It was apparent that they all believed I was an impostor, an interloper, a Westerner invading their peace.

"But look at my passport," I said desperately, showing the blue badge of privilege.

The old man stared at the photograph and name. "Omer . . . Umar . . . Umer . . . This is a Muslim name . . ." He looked confused, as though I was trying to deceive him.

Suddenly, the man's eyes grew wide and he pointed a finger upward. "Recite!" he claimed. "Recite the *Shahadah*!" He was asking me to state the declaration of faith, the single sentence of Arabic text, known to all Muslims, attesting that there was no god but God, and Muhammad was His Messenger. It was literally written above our heads on the walls of the mosque.

I recited it quickly, stumbling through the words, my voice choking.

The old man shook his head. I had made a mistake in my pronunciation.

"Recite," he said. "Recite."

Now I was surrounded by more people. Terrified, I fell silent. I was ready to flee, just like I had done in the days of my youth from the boys on the block. I felt shame. Here was the one place I thought I would be welcomed, and yet it was also here that I felt most like a stranger.

I turned to leave, hating myself for failing to convince my own people that I was one of theirs. Several older women, their heads covered, came to see what the commotion was. They looked from my face to the old man's and smiled to themselves, patiently explaining to him that there had been a misunderstanding.

"Let the brother in," one of the women said.

The old man, realizing he had made an error, turned to me. "You young men have gone into evil ways," he said. "You have become hostages to false gods, have become too Westernized. You have lost your faith and lost your history."

I nodded along with his lecture, even though I wondered whether the West was not my true home. When the crowd dispersed, I felt rage: unable to belong anywhere, forced to show my papers everywhere, yearning for some community of my own. But I had sympathy for the old man, who could have been my grandfather,

7

a man living under occupation and accustomed to Westerners strolling through this ancient plateau like they owned it.

Outside the mosque, I heard shouts and chants. An even greater disturbance was beginning.

"*Allahu Akbar!*" the voices shouted. Other voices responded in Hebrew. The security guards moved past me to see, and before my eyes, I watched as Jewish settlers and Palestinian residents squared off in the distance: the West and the East, clashing. As the chaos grew around me, I found myself once again caught in the middle.

Everywhere I went there had been an implicit question everyone seemed to be asking: What side are you on? It should have been an easy question to answer, given that English was my first language, that I was born to a working-class immigrant family in North America, and the journey I went on took me from a little corner of Toronto to Paris, Cambridge, Yale Law School, places I believed would allow for my rebirth as a true Westerner. Over time, I had been transformed into someone I no longer recognized. Over time, my mask had disfigured my face.

I stood at the entrance of the mosque with brown skin and an empty stomach, and it was there, amid the torrent of hurt and fear, that the reality of running from myself, being rendered invisible, marked as an outsider, defined by others, and forced to confront the coldness of the human heart in all its forms—it was only then that the wounds opened up the past, and the story returned to me.

I.
Origins

1.

Northern Winter

O nce upon a time in the colder days of my childhood, right before the new millennium, I found myself in our family bungalow watching the snow fall and dreaming of running away. Though the temperatures outside had dropped below freezing, and a snowy dust drifted over the sidewalks and cars, it felt like the world around me was on fire.

I was nine years old and waiting with terror because my father would soon be home and would ask to see my report card. Grades were important to him, even though neither of my parents had academic degrees. My father's temper was volcanic and could explode at any moment, so the house was often tense. I usually retreated into my daydreaming and imagination when things got too loud. The outside world dazzled me with its mysteries. Had any of the neighbors seen me seeing them, they would have spotted a roundheaded boy with big eyes, a buzz cut, and a Power Rangers shirt on, observing the world through his window.

Fog formed on the glass where I exhaled. I wrote my name out in Urdu the way my grandmother had taught me, three letters, the name of the second caliph to succeed the Prophet Muhammad. Some of the houses under the white snow had lights flickering to mark the holiday, the birth of Christ, but our home was darkened. It should have been a happy time, but Christmas was always the loneliest evening of the year.

I imagined myself opening the window and running away to some magical place, an adventure beyond the confines of this house. I wondered if I could fly through the heavens like the Prophet Muhammad, on a winged horse. Staring out at the blizzard, I wondered what lay beyond this neighborhood. I was a curious, imaginative child, but beneath this wonder, I was also deeply afraid. After my father came home, at any moment there could be a verbal brawl. And I knew that when he got home, he would find out I had done poorly at school, and a beating was inevitable.

Our home was in Scarborough, a suburb on the easternmost edge of Toronto. When my father, whom I called Dada because I could not pronounce "Dad," read his *Toronto Star*, he noted that Scarborough was always described by its gangs, its shootings, stabbings, and immigrant families. The world outside the house could be menacing, but I was more afraid of my father. Maybe this year would be different than all the others. Maybe there was hope. My ears, attuned to all the sounds around me, had heard the elders whispering about the midnight hour, that when the clock struck twelve, the world would come to an end—*Armageddon*, a boy at school had said. I didn't want the world to end—but if it was going to end, this was a good year for it to happen.

I felt a tap on my shoulder, my reverie broken. I turned to see my mother ready to scold me. Amma had long black hair, warm eyes, and was wearing the customary shalwar kameez. She had been cooking, the onions making her eyes water as she wiped a tear with her dupatta.

"Have you said your prayers?" she asked in Urdu.

"Not yet," I said.

"Go say them now. Allah doesn't like when we are late in saying our prayers. Quickly, before your father comes home."

Amma never referred to my father by his name. In Urdu she used the word *Aap*, a term of respect. When other people were around, she called him *voh*, which was like saying "they." I spoke only Urdu with Amma. With my father, I spoke only English. I switched back and forth between the two languages with ease, but my thoughts were always in English.

I said goodbye to the snow and turned away from the window. My grandmother was sitting at her usual spot on the couch.

"Come fix this *kambakht* TV," Dadiye said, cursing.

I went to the tiny box and gave it a shake. A VCR was underneath, which could play our *Lion King* cassette. The small living room had a crimson Pakistani carpet, black-and-white photographs of relatives with stern looks on their faces, calligraphy from the Qur'an on the wall. Dadiye sat regally with a blanket on her lap, her hair dyed jet-black, occupying the couch like it was a throne. Dadiye was my father's mother, our matriarch, and had been living with us since the beginning of time. She was my favorite person in the house because she never asked me to pray and took me and my brother to McDonald's on the weekend. Dadiye's routine was the same: chai at ten a.m., followed by afternoon prayer, then watching Oprah and calling relatives back home, demanding to know every detail of gossip, managing the extended clan in Pakistan like an empress tending to her colonies. Amma's relationship with Dadiye was respectful but tense, and I learned to play the women off each other, going between them like a boy diplomat whenever their silent treatments went on for days.

Dadiye liked to sit me down and tell me tales about the past. She said that when angels came down from the heavens, they took our good deeds and bad deeds and reported them back to Allah. She said that the Prophet Muhammad had received his first revelation in a cave from the Angel Jibra'eel.

"How many wings did the angel have?" I asked her.

"Six hundred," she said.

Dadiye coughed. She had just recovered from pneumonia. "There was a time, long ago," she said, "when our people were kings and princes. We were maharajas and ranis and shahs and kings and queens. We lived in peace with Sikhs and Hindus in India. My brother, your great-uncle—there is his portrait, with the white mustache—he was a doctor in London. He met the viceroy. We were once very respected. Did you know that long ago . . ."

The what? The who? If we were so great, why did the heater not work? What relevance did "back then" have to the snowstorms of Toronto on an unquiet Christmas night? I didn't know what to make of her tales. Dadiye would begin such stories and then cut them off, as though the gaps had been deliberately left for me to fill. She had tried to convey that there had been a long life for her and the family before Toronto—a life that went back to Pakistan, and before that to British India, stories that she, and my parents, had left behind. They were myths that had mingled with memory and I never quite believed them.

I went to the room where my brother was sleeping. His name was Oz and he was one year younger than me and everything I was not: dutiful, good at school, responsible. My father said I should be more like him, and this made me care even less about school. He was so innocent that once he asked our father what a condom was on the way to the YMCA, before I pinched his legs until he squealed.

I laid out the prayer mat, raised my palms to my ears, and said, "*Allahu Akbar.*" I stood facing the East, facing Mecca, falling to my knees in prostration, and afterward sat on the prayer mat and upturned my palms to the ceiling. I prayed just like Amma had taught me and asked Allah to bless me and help me get good grades. I asked Allah if it was true that He was going to make the world end and whether I would be burned in the hellfire, the dreaded *dozakh*, that was described in a million different details that made me shudder. It was the holy month of Ramadan and Amma made Oz and me fast that month. She had said that the angels gathered every child's prayers and took them to Allah during these thirty days. She said even the trees prostrated to God on the holiest nights. I thought I should take advantage of this opportunity.

"Dear Allah," I whispered with firm conviction, "please make me a rapper." I waited, then spoke again. "Dear Allah, send Santa Claus to our house this year. Make Dada forget about my report card. Don't let them all go crazy tonight. *Ameen.*"

It was then that I heard the front door blow open with force. I quickly put the mat away. Dada was home.

"*Omer! Osman! Outside Now!*" he shouted.

It was a known rule never to delay when our father called. Dada's

15

face would go red, his eyes would widen, his temple veins would bulge as he exploded in anger. I looked to my younger brother Oz drooling in his sleep and thought whether to wake him up. Better to let him dream and go help our father on my own.

Dada was waiting for me by the door. He was short with broad shoulders and a handsome face, wearing a rumpled coat that had a giant "P" sign emblazoned on the front. He had on a Soviet-style winter cap that made him look like a brown Joseph Stalin. Flecks of snow clung to his mustache. I knew Dada was a parking officer who worked all winter and slapped tickets on car windshields, but at home he called himself an "officer of the law."

Grunting, Dada went outside. I followed behind, waddling like a penguin in an oversized winter coat. The snowfall had grown thicker.

We were supposed to shovel together, but there was only one shovel and two of us, so I watched Dada work while he yelled.

"Don't be a *kamchor*," he said, meaning a work-thief. "Laziness will keep you back in this world. Here, do like this, like this." He pushed a mound of snow away from the door. "See how I throw the snow? I use gravity to help me. I *throw* the snow. You have to use your brain, don't be a dummy, use some force."

As Dada threw the snow, he continued his exhortation. "Insurance companies . . . banks . . . politicians . . . none of them are your friends, remember. They only want to put the hand in the pocket. They are crooks."

I nodded, pretending to understand. Down the street, I could hear the cargo train growling down the tracks.

"You guys," he said, "you have the best of everything. When I was growing up in Pakistan, I had nothing. I had to feed the chick-

16

ens, walk ten miles to school, take care of parents, cook for family, do my studies. You have everything. Am I right?"

It was always phrased as a question, forcing me—and my brother, when we were together—to assent. The one time I said, "No," I was slapped. I stayed silent, exhaling white clouds of breath, curious about what the chickens in Pakistan had to do with the snows in Canada.

Dada exploded curse words like a cannon. "*Matharchod!* Use some force! Some power!" I couldn't tell whether he was cursing me, himself, or his shovel.

After we finished shoveling snow, we went back inside the house together. I saw the two women, Amma and Dadiye, sitting on the sofa, drinking chai and giving each other death stares. They had a tense rivalry, a competition between daughter-in-law and mother-in-law, always on the verge of dispute.

"Tahir," Dadiye said to my father. "Relax or your blood pressure will go up."

"Let it go up!" he said.

"*Chalo,*" she said, and reverted to Punjabi. I didn't understand Punjabi, but Dadiye had uttered something about how no one listened to her.

I saw my father fiddling with a plastic bag. He took out a little Christmas tree, a smile on his face.

"Tonight," Dada proclaimed, "we will celebrate *the* Christmas."

I hid my excitement. Christmas was usually a sad week for me because we never celebrated. At school, we sang carols and exchanged gifts and everyone was merry, but at home I had come to believe that Santa Claus did not visit people like us.

Amma frowned.

"Why do you wish to copy these traditions?" she asked him in Urdu. "It is Ramadan, you do not fast. We have our own holidays, like Eid, it is coming up. The children are learning not to care about their roots. They are becoming *pukka Angrez*."

Dada retorted, "Jesus is our prophet, too. Look at how Christians built the modern world. We should learn from them."

"Jews do not celebrate Christmas," Amma said.

"I am Jewish," Dada retorted. "Look at how Jewish people take care of each other, build schools, become doctors. What do we do? Only build madrassas in every town."

"Ji," Amma said. "Christmas is for the Christians. They cele-brate . . . the birth of . . . the birth of God!"

I knew she had touched a nerve, for the greatest sin in our religion was *shirk*, or associating partners with the one God.

"I am Christian," Dada said. "We must *integ*-rate, Salma. We must adopt these traditions! This is our country! Otherwise we will be stuck in our past."

Dada had gone red in the face. I could feel another argument about to erupt.

Between husband and wife, grandmother now intervened. Dadiye gestured to me and, in her flair for drama, pronounced a matriarch's firm rebuke.

"They will forget everything," Dadiye said. "You will see. When kids are born and raised here, they forget their roots. This is the *gora*'s land, remember."

Amma responded to this sacred challenge, younger woman to older. "Your children may have forgotten everything, but mine will remember."

What were they so angry about? Why was their passion so intense? They weren't arguing about Christmas trees or lights or Santa Claus anymore—they were fighting about so much more, about heritage and tradition, culture and religion, and how to raise me and my two brothers, Oz and Ali, the latter still a baby, in the country where we were born but that they had migrated to only recently. The past, present, and future were enmeshed in conflict.

As the screams grew louder, I covered my ears and ran toward the bathroom. I shut the door and crouched down by the toilet. Here, alone, I was safe.

Vicious words were uttered outside the door in Urdu, a poetic tongue, which made the words more poisonous.

Matharchod!

Thief!

Sinner!

Drinker!

Hellfire!

From a mud hut!

Bring the Qur'an!

A shattering silence.

If it wasn't for my hard work, we'd still be in the projects!

I had been warned by my parents not to make friends with kids from "broken homes." As the shouts grew feverish outside the door, I wondered if we weren't broken, too.

Long into the night, the elders fought. They sounded merciless, as if they had been arguing this way not for ten years but a hundred years. They were carrying wounds I could not fathom, stories I had not yet discovered. Past lives and remembrances that they held with desperation, tempers exploding because none of their pain could be put into words. I did not understand that the anguish they carried was tied to a deeper story of leaving their pasts behind, reinventing themselves in a cold and distant country. They were growing up in a new world, just like I was, unanchored souls without a secure life. Though migration could be full of beautiful journeys, there was also a bitterness at the heart of the experience. Bitterness and violence. Families were citadels of memory, connecting stories to future generations—but the chain had been broken along the way, and could be redeemed only in the children.

The shouts grew louder. The sound of thunder, a blitzkrieg of broken plates. I covered my ears. I hid. I dreamt of escape.

When the battle ended, it turned out the little Christmas tree didn't even work.

. . .

Ten years before our nightly family duels, on another winter day, a plane landed at Toronto Pearson Airport. Among the migrants and travelers and visitors was my mother, Salma, who was leaving her family in Pakistan to join the man she had married in Canada.

She was twenty-nine, a teacher who loved her students, setting out for the new world. The bitter cold stung her face, the wind sharp as needles. But stepping onto the tarmac, the woman, whose beauty was noted by all the locals of her community, was reminded of the snowfalls in her village in Pakistan, a place called Murree, up in the mountains where the kids made snow forts and snowmen during their own winter days.

On her mind was the village left behind and the new country

that was to be sacralized by the word *home.* The strange sounds of English would have to be learned, the tasteless food adjusted to, and the mannerisms of this frigid city deciphered. She had come to Canada only two years before I was born, rupturing the tight-knit family she had loved. Now everything was new. She was a stranger with a young family.

My father had immigrated in the 1970s and was studying at a community college while working odd jobs. His first name was Tahir, the eldest of three children born right after Pakistan became independent. A child of the city Lahore, he knew the world better than my mother. When Dada arrived in Toronto, he was part of that great movement of peoples brought on by the opening of immigration laws in Canada and the United States. Like migrants before him, Dada struggled first with his name. The white people of his new country could not pronounce *Tahir*, so they called him *Tire*. They could not pronounce his middle name, *Mian*, so they called him *Mr. Man*. Aziz was rhymed with *disease*, and other slurs and cusses were spoken, some replied to but most unanswered, the second looks and backhanded comments internalized into his combustible temperament. But Dada was a man who took nothing from no one and believed he was as good as any white man. Fed up with his name being slandered, he did what many immigrants before him had done and took on an entirely new name. From that day forward, Tahir was known as "Miami."

When Dada was still a student, his father in Pakistan passed suddenly from a heart attack. The duties of manhood were passed on to him overnight, and he quit school to become the sole bread-winner for the family. He worked as a waiter, serving the powerful white men of the city as they spent more money on a single meal than Dada earned in an entire month. Next, he walked through the snow asking anyone who might listen for a job. One day, he saw an officer in a white uniform, went up to him, and asked to know what he did. A few weeks later, Dada was hired as a parking officer, and for the next fifty years he walked across Toronto, ensuring no one had parked illegally. He sent money back home so his relatives would not starve, and used his savings to bring my widowed grandmother, Dadiye, to Canada.

Whereas Dada came from the city, Amma came from the countryside. Rural and landless peasant folk lived in those mountains of Murree. The people of her village had the features of northernly warriors: tall, light brown skin, sharp green eyes. They spoke a dialect called Pahari, and families lived and raised children together, passing on their ancestral traditions.

Tensions crippled their marriage from the start; Dada expected a quiet Muslim wife, but Amma saw herself as his equal, fierce in her own right, and wishing to preserve her heritage. She was not the docile, reserved woman she seemed to be, and this led to quarrels between my mother and father and my mother and grandmother.

It was a strange union: the wife being religious, the husband being secular; the wife resisting the pull of assimilation, the husband rushing to assimilate and discard his prior identity. Theirs was not what some modern types in the community now call "a love marriage"; it was arranged, pure and simple. Marriage was considered too grave and serious a matter to be left to the whims of children. The contract between past and future was to be preserved by the elders, passed on for posterity, made sacred in the union of marriage.

When I was three, Amma took me and my brother to Pakistan. We met our cousins and relatives, but I remembered nothing from the trip. She told me that her village was part of my roots, and in our home she was fiercely protective of her family's origins—especially when my father belittled them and said she came from "a mud hut."

As I grew up in the chaos of a household constantly at war with itself, I learned to be hypervigilant of my surroundings. Omens and warnings were around me. Evil eyes above me. Shame, *sharam*, within me. Six of us were crammed into our small household: along with my father, mother, and grandmother there were my two younger brothers, Osman and Ali—Oz one year younger, and Ali just two. Coincidentally, the three of us were named after the caliphs who had succeeded the Prophet, men we were taught to revere, but whose real stories were deeply tragic. Three generations stuffed together in a forgotten corner of Canada, with cockroaches in the kitchen, a beat-up Pontiac in the driveway, and an oldest son about to come of age in the new millennium.

Over sleepless nights, I lay in the bedroom and stared up at the cold darkness, watching the moon shining past the trees, feeling alone and terrified. As the snow fell faintly, I closed my eyes and imagined another world, one beyond the highways and fields, waiting for me, if only I could reach it. If only I could escape this northern winter.

2.

Scartown

Guests rarely came over to our house unless it was Eid, the Muslim holiday. Dada and Dadiye had disputes within the family, and the relatives were experts at giving each other years-long silent treatments. On Eid, though, everyone enacted a truce.

Early in the morning, Dada, wearing a kurta, took me and my brother Oz to the mosque for prayer. When we returned, Amma and Dadiye were at the door, ready to share sweets. We wished each other "Eid Mubarak," and hugged three times. Dadiye slipped a ten-dollar bill in my palm, her yearly gift.

By late afternoon, family members began showing up at our door wearing bright colors. I wore the cream kurta Amma had laid out for me. She had been in the kitchen all night cooking. Braids of steam rose through the house, and the living room had the delicious scent of chicken karahi. Soon, the little house was full of auntees and uncles jostling for food, gossiping about who so-and-so had married, and talking loudly about politics.

The doorbell rang. I ran to the front door and saw one of my auntees, whom we called Baji. This was my father's sister, a thin woman with a shrill voice and short black hair, who was always hyper.

"Getting fat again, *heina*?" she said, pulling my ear.

"No, Auntee," I replied.

Baji scrunched her face in contempt. "*No Auntee*," she said, mocking my English. "*Bas na? Urdu bolo.*" Enough. Speak Urdu.

"I will," I said, lying as I walked away.

Soon, all the uncles gathered in the living room to discuss important matters like the price of cable packages and who had put an illegal dish on the roof. Dada sat there with his legs wide apart, hunched over as he provoked the other uncles. The conversation turned to politics, urgent matters of war and peace, the uncles holding teacups in their hands and their bellies in their laps, gesturing not like they were in the Toronto suburbs but in the White House Situation Room.

I sat among them, trying to understand.

Said one uncle: "Pakistan is a nuclear-armed state being kept down by the greedy Western powers."

A second uncle spoke. "*Amreeka* has a plan to dominate Afghanistan and Pakistan."

Another uncle, an oval-shaped man named Iqbal Mian, liked to preach about religion and politics. He had a thick mustache that he twisted while speaking.

"The Indian prime minister," Iqbal Mian said solemnly, "drinks a cup of his own urine every morning."

All the other uncles nodded in agreement. A round of ritualistic India-bashing and Pakistan-promoting continued for some minutes. The only subject they could agree on was that India might invade them. I looked to my father, who shook his head. I felt small and ignorant listening to them, the big men talking about world events I could not fathom. I wondered why they were so passionate about things happening thousands of miles from us, in a place I did not even know.

Dada was in his element during these debates. He barreled at the uncles with inquisition and rebuttal, losing his temper, probing them as though the fate of the world hung on the discussion. He said outlandish things just to stir them up.

"We Pakistanis barely deserve a country," he said. "Westerners are putting men on the moon while we argue about whether our pants fall below our ankles!"

Iqbal Mian twirled his mustache.

"Do you see what is happening in Peshawar?" my father asked.

The uncles would share stories of specific people in different towns and cities—Lahore, Islamabad, Murree, Karachi. But their conversation always returned to religion and its role in our life.

"We Mussulmaan should follow the way of the Prophet, peace be upon him, in all matters," Iqbal Mian said.

In these conversations, I knew it was tradition for at least one uncle to try to out-Islam the others. But Dada did not play by the rules.

"What does that mean?" Dada asked.

Iqbal Mian picked at his teeth. "It means I follow the Prophet, peace be upon him, and do everything he did."

Dada said, "Prophet rode a camel. You drive a truck."

"That was then."

Dada said, "Prophet lived in seventh century. We live in the twenty-first century."

"So what?" Iqbal Mian asked.

"Prophet had nine wives. You have one *begum*."

"And?"

"And," Dada said, holding back laughter, "Prophet was the Messenger of Allah. You, Mian Sahab, are a security guard."

Iqbal Mian adjusted his kurta and picked at his teeth. The conversation went on this way for an hour, before the uncles exhausted themselves. When the women joined in—they were in the kitchen, engaged in their own conversations—the uncles calmed down.

Suddenly, Iqbal Mian glared at me. The other uncles looked as well—the scolding about to unite them all.

"Omer needs to live a practical life," Iqbal Mian said.

"His head is in the clouds," another uncle said.

"Send him to Pakistan. That will fix him," said another.

But I did not want to be "fixed." I wanted to live my own life, out in the world—a life that, even as a boy, I felt my elders had no clue about.

Dada listened patiently before striking back. "Don't you all worry. My boy can become anything he wants in life. Even if he wishes to be an actor, that is okay."

An actor? I thought.

The uncles got back to discussing religion, and I hazily heard my father ask something about India or America, setting off another loud debate. Those early Eid discussions were my initiation into the world of politics, into the idea that there was a larger universe outside our street, and that events far away were somehow linked to our personal lives. I understood only dimly that my elders were connected to distant lands with their own politics and histories, faraway places with histories and names I did not know.

Brown Boy

...

Our home was in Scartown. That's what the kids called Scarborough, that distant part of Toronto where no one wanted to live. A working-class, inner suburb on the edge of the city that had once been called Scarberia because of how far away it was, cut off like a remote island. Back when Dada immigrated here, the borough was filled with working-class white people. They began moving out as the immigrants and refugees moved in. Now the residents were mostly Black, Brown, and Asian. And it wasn't called Scarberia anymore—none of us would have understood the reference.

Stepping outside my front door, I entered the vortex of the neighborhood. Overhead power lines, crumbling streets that went on for eternity, browned-out apartments and towering projects. Endless strip malls and Indian and Arab stores. Around the corner: a halal butcher, the local Karachi Bazaar where we bought our spices, Hakka Chinese restaurants. The sounds of my street were a symphony of tongues: Jamaican patois mixed with Hindi, African American English, Arabic, Bengali, Tamil.

I crossed a bridge over a swamp to get to school. The first thing I saw were the boys lined up by the fence: Black boys, Brown kids, white kids. Most of my friends were Black and Brown, children with obscure origins and from places like Jaffa or Kingston or Port of Spain. We spoke in a slang the teachers did not understand. We listened to hip-hop and did not censor the words. Leaving home, I would assume a new costume, of the boy who just wanted to fit in and pretend he did not speak Urdu with his mother, pretend that his parents were not from Pakistan, because the white boys had a special slur for us.

School was the inverse of home. Though I did not care about my studies, I felt I could be anyone at school, as long as no one brought up my ethnic heritage. School was a sort of imprisoning freedom, just being out of the house and in another building. But I saw no purpose to school, and was uninterested in anything the teachers had to say. The worst sort of apathetic student: one who is naturally curious but has learned to keep his mouth shut. A lost cause.

The only space of pure enjoyment was the basketball court, pickup games at recess and lunch that were played with the fervor of fanatics. Ball was religion, hope, and a dream all at once. On that cracked concrete court, we became superstars. Every boy wanted to glide through the air like Vince Carter, the Toronto Raptors star, who soared as if performing aerial ballet. He and Kobe Bryant were the only heroes we had, and every boy hollered out *"Kobe!"* while taking a jump shot—knees bent, proper form, wrist release, and the flashing lights of the big stage in our eyes.

At school, I did my best to blend in. My closest friend was a boy born in Guyana who had grown up in Scartown. His name was Shilton Lutchman and he embodied his last name like a comedian, calling himself "Deh Lunchman." Shilton had lush brown skin, poetic eyes, and a smile that he flashed at anyone who might pass. He made everyone laugh. When I got to school after a rough argument at home, Shilton could make me forget about my parents in a second. I had a love for this boy, the way his bright durag fell past his shoulders, the way he sang Usher tracks and rapped West

Indian lyrics. Riding on a purple bike to school, he'd pull up close to me and ask, "Wha'gwan wich you?" I was comfortable with Shilton because I knew he would not judge me or force me to be anyone other than who I already was.

And I knew my parents, like the parents of many Pakistani and Indian kids, did not approve of us being friends with Black boys, even Black boys who ate daal at home and watched Bollywood movies. More than once, an auntee had told me in the summer, "You've gotten so *black*," and it was not a compliment. This made me like Shilton even more, made me gravitate further toward the culture the Black kids carried with them like talismans. For Shilton's roots, like those of most of the West Indians here, went back to both Africa and India. I did not understand how that was possible, but history was obscured in school: the white people had come to North America and traded furs and everything was lovely ever after. Perhaps this was the real reason I paid no attention at school: I had the child's aptitude to detect when he is being bullshitted.

As soon as the bell rang, I became sullen and withdrawn. I wanted to be invisible at school, to hide away from the white kids. I had learned to be afraid of white people from before I learned the alphabet. After a white girl asked me why my lunch looked like poo I began throwing out the lunches Amma made for me every day. It's almost clichéd, the lunch being thrown away, yet in those early years, it meant a growling stomach and a building resentment as the hours passed and I went hungry.

One day in fifth grade, we were learning alliteration, and our teacher asked us to list words that began with the same sound as our name. I played with my pencil. I engraved my initials in my desk.

I wrote bad poetry and bad rap lyrics. I didn't even like my own name, *Omer*. The name morphed depending on where I happened to be. At home, it was pronounced *Uhmur*. At school, the teachers called me *O-mar* and I did not correct them.

"Um, dear," the teacher said, "do you need some help?"

I shook my head.

"But you haven't written anything."

I shrugged. "I don't know any words that start with the letter *O*."

The teacher, who had brown hair and a grandmotherly face, brought over a giant book. I had never seen such a book—had never opened any books outside of school. I distrusted her the way I distrusted all my teachers. She opened the book and pointed to the letter *O*, and there were dozens and dozens of words.

"How about this word?" she asked.

I tried to spell it out. "O-b-s-e-r-v-a-n-t."

"Very good," she said. "You have potential. You just must try, dear, try harder."

When we went around the class, the Charismatic Christinas and Proud Pauls triumphantly gave their alliteration examples. I said mine in a murmur. "Observant Omer." I sat down, head down, eyes down, relieved no one asked me any questions.

School served no purpose I could see. Because when the bell rang and we were let out, I was faced with the same neighborhood, watching my back and avoiding the tough kids. The white boys were prone to use slurs. *Paki* was their favorite racial insult. Even at the age of ten, I knew this word to be derogatory because it felt like a dagger in my skin. *Paki*—not shorthand for "Pakistani," but a racial slur that started with neo-Nazis in England. None of us kids knew the etymology of this epithet, but we all knew it was a vile insult, and that nothing could be said in return. The white boys were the only ones with the language to provoke our shame. That was their power.

Our teachers liked to say we lived in a multicultural country, but that multiculturalism, on the ground, was still deformed, and full of subtle hatreds. I didn't know all this. I felt it. I was afraid of being seen with my mother, who could be insulted for wearing a shalwar kameez. I was frightened of smelling like spices. I was terrified of being seen as a Paki. My childhood brain was only focused at all hours on keeping my English unaccented, my heritage undetected, my color unseen.

...

Knowing that I was doing poorly in class, I still opened my report card with tense nerves. I wanted to assess the damage before my father found out. Some tiny part of me hoped, in the seconds before I ripped open the tan envelope, that the grades might be decent. But they were never good. The bad marks hurt at first, then became normal. D– in math. D in science. C– in English. Only a B– in gym.

My grades were an embarrassment at home, especially because my younger brother Oz was getting straight As.

"Be more like your brother," Dada would say. "Look at him, he studies and is doing well in the *maths*. He is going to have a job one day. You will stay a flunky."

But I kept spacing out in class, daydreaming.

A few days after we learned alliteration, I was on the ball court. I swiped the basketball away from a white boy named Kyle. He had freckles and light brown eyes and buckteeth, and though he was failing even worse than I was, I couldn't help but notice how the teachers gave him second and third chances, were impressed by the fact that he played hockey.

I was guarding Kyle that day. He was double-dribbling, going out-of-bounds, breaking every rule of the game—and getting away with it.

Kyle pushed me backward. I tumbled and stood up. He walked to me and threw his body at mine.

"Stop it!" I shouted. "What are you doing?"

"You think you're tough?" he asked.

I looked around. Play had stopped and now everyone was watching us. I did not want to fight. I was scared and wanted to hide or run. But I knew this was my test and if I failed now, nothing I did inside the classroom would matter.

"You play ball like that in your country, pussy?" he said, laughing.

I went red. I did not know what to say.

"Fuck you," I shouted.

Kyle kept smiling, laughing, a laughter I was to know well.

"Let me ask you something," he said. "What are you?"

"What do you mean?" I asked.

"I'm asking, what *are* you?"

But before I could answer, he said, "You aren't white. No matter how hard you try, you'll always be a Paki."

The word slashed through me. *Paki, Paki, Paki, Paki, Paki.* I saw the white girls laughing. I saw the Black kids looking away as if they wanted no part in this game.

Tears welled up in my eyes. I wished there was a word I could use against him that would make Kyle cry, but this language we were speaking was his before it was mine. There was no slur to use in self-defense. My father's first lesson was never to cry in public, but all I wanted to do was run to a corner and hide my face. I felt the shame of who I was, ashamed of my parents, ashamed of my own skin.

Suddenly, I began to feel angry. As Kyle smirked and got closer, I pushed him away. He grabbed my shoulder, pulled my shirt. He swung his fist toward my face. I was shaken, but lunged forward and kicked him. I punched and flayed and cried and scratched, tears falling down my face, blindly throwing my fists in every direction.

When I got home, I was cut and bleeding from my elbows and hands. My face had dirt smeared on it. My shirt was ripped. Even after fighting that boy, I felt sick to my stomach. I had caused pain to another human being and I wanted no part in the violence.

Amma was mortified. "What happened to you?" she asked.

I said nothing, went to my room and lay my aching body down.

Paki, Paki, Paki, Paki, Paki rang in my ears.

Amma tried to soothe me. But I hated her in that moment—hated how she prayed, hated how she spoke English, hated the fact that her and my father's origins gave the white kids ammunition against me. When Dada got home, he found out what happened and came into the room. I ducked under the covers.

"Get up," he said.

Reluctantly, I stood. I hated him, too, and the fact that he knew I had not defended myself well.

"Did you try to be peaceful at first?" he asked.

I nodded.

He examined my face, the cuts and bruises.

"What's the matter with you, then? Why can't you hit those boys back? No one in this world will respect you if you can't fight back."

I tried to say something, tried to tell him that I was afraid of getting hurt.

"I don't care about your excuses. You stand up and be a man. Anyone touches you, lay them on their ass. Bite, scratch, kick them in the balls if you must. The world will rip you apart and throw you to the dogs if you are weak."

I could feel the tears in my eyes.

"Look at me," he said. I wanted to look away. "I am going to teach you to defend yourself. Next time, don't come home beaten up unless you throw a few more punches yourself."

This was the first lesson I took from childhood. That some people were going to hate me just because of who I was, and I would have to fight or flee. I was young and innocent and did not like violence. But this was the cauldron into which I was born, and I had to sharpen my eyes to the realities around me, keep my hands ready to defend myself, be quick on my toes in case I had to run, and always be listening for the subtle change of tone that could signal coming aggression. An enormous amount of mental energy went into surviving, blending in, being invisible—and my real education had scarcely begun.

3.

Phantoms and Ghosts

The core of our household was our religion, and religion was firmly in my mother's hands. Not even my father questioned her power in this domain. The kitchen was Amma's first kingdom, but her true sovereignty lay over matters of faith. Soon after the world did not end, Amma had begun talking about enrolling me and my brother at the local mosque. I always thought she was just bluffing.

One evening I was at the dinner table doing math problems when Amma came around the corner, fixed her dupatta, and said:

"I will be putting you and your brother into the local masjid. There you can learn Qur'an and learn about your religion."

I had no interest in going to the masjid.

"Please, no!" I implored.

She had already taught me how to pray and told me stories about the Prophet Muhammad. We had gone to the local Scartown mosque a few times, and each time I felt overwhelmed by the prayer and silence. *Recite!* was the first revelation the Prophet had received, my mother told us. *Recite*, or *Read!* Muhammad, sitting in the cave where the archangel had appeared to him, had answered, *But I cannot read.* It was then that the Qur'an began to be revealed.

I did not know any of the history between the Prophet's revelation and our own time. The Islamic past was not shared in our household—fourteen hundred years of politics and science and development were not known, nor was the violence. Islam was the oxygen we breathed, shaping all the rules I grew up with. Alcohol was haram. Pork was untouchable. Another brother or sister was to be greeted with As-salamu alaykum. The Jews and Christians were the People of the Book, their religions to be respected as forerunners to our own. My brother and I would line up in our home and pray the Salaat with my mother, one of us reciting the Azan, or call to prayer, and facing toward the East. Amma taught us that the first muezzin, or person proclaiming the prayer call, was a former slave named Bilal. She taught us that in our faith, honesty and decency were the most important—especially toward those who were less fortunate than us.

Religion bound us to one another. Religion lived within us. But religion, the way it was taught by elders and reinforced at the mosque, was all about fear. You had to be afraid. Deeply terrified: of the end of times. Of the Final Day, *Qiyamat*. Of the punishments we sinners would face. Of the lashes in hell, the fires burning skin, fires a thousand times hotter than the fires on earth. Hell was the ending and the beginning. The real fun started when the angel visited the person who had just died for a full interrogation about their life.

"Pray or the djinn will find you," an auntee told me. "Shaytaan"— Satan—"does not like when you eat with your left hand." The threat of eternal punishment hovered over my shoulder. So my imagination went to plenty of dark places. I was mortified of the hellfire, of evil spirits, of smokeless beings, of Satan himself—and my young brain suspected that I was one of the bad people, the sinners, who would burn in hell, in *dozakh*.

In my mind and heart, I was a boy haunted by phantoms and ghosts.

Despite my protests, starting in middle school, my brother Oz and I began attending classes at the local mosque, Monday to Friday, for two hours every evening after school. We donned a shalwar kameez and skullcap and carried our Qur'ans with us. I did not want to go, but in matters of faith I had no choice. My mother was adamant as ever that her boys learn about their roots. After I got home from school and Amma finished her babysitting shift—a job she was doing on the side to make a little extra money—we went to the mosque. Amma started by taking us on the bus—a trip I hated because I thought the other people on the bus knew we were going to the masjid. After Dada bought a used minivan, Amma started driving us, which didn't stop me from slinking down in my seat when we drove through my neighborhood—especially when Amma made me wear a skullcap.

Abu Bakr Masjid was a small white building with a minaret, at the end of an unpaved lot. It was next to the Tower Blocks, a set of public housing projects that dotted the landscape of Scartown. Pakistani and Indian shops were across the street. The entrance to the mosque was simple, unadorned.

I walked inside the masjid that first day, a young boy entering an uncertain world. I saw shoes scattered all over the lobby. A long row of washing tubs was off to the side, and I saw giant men sitting on stools, leaning forward and washing themselves. They were performing the *Wudhu*, a ritual ablution that was necessary before touching the Qur'an or praying. I stared as each man, uncles with beards, sleeves rolled up, washed himself more vigorously than the next. The whole area was flooded when it was my turn.

Entering the main hall with its green carpet and low ceiling, I heard a hundred young voices chanting verses from the Qur'an. The spiritual cadences of these 1,400-year-old verses made my ears sing. Dozens of classes were in session, students sitting at little tables on the floor, rocking back and forth, waiting to deliver their recitation. At the head of every class was the dreaded *maulvi sahib*, or religious teacher. They wore long kurtas, had beards of varying lengths, the more ancient men having orange beards dyed with *mehndi*, or henna. I was afraid of the maulvis as soon as I saw one of them slap a boy for messing up his verses.

The maulvi whose class I joined was a chubby grandfather named Mullanna Fazlur-Rehman. He had a lined face worn out by age, white hair, a cannonball belly over which his kurta stretched. Mullanna Fazlur-Rehman aggressively ran his fingers through his beard, stroking and pulling the hairs and then flicking them away, nodding in anticipation as students recited.

The women and girls prayed behind a drape that hung from a makeshift iron rod. We boys did not know what happened behind this Iron Curtain, but I was always curious. When Amma picked me up in the evening, I tried to glimpse the women in their abayas and hijabs, walking out of the mosque toward the Tower Blocks. Theirs was a forbidden world.

Over the next few months, a routine developed. On the way to the mosque, I practiced my assigned verses, then sat at my little table and recited some more. An hour later Mullanna Fazlur-Rehman called my name and I nervously went to the front and sat down before him, took a deep breath, and opened the holy book. I trembled while reciting these verses whose meanings I did not understand, because out of the corner of my eye, I could see the maulvi's chubby finger drumming against the edge of the table, waiting for a mistake, his ring finger *tap-tap-tapping* against the wood.

Suddenly, his hand came up and struck me. I ducked. He tried again. I moved back. We spent the next few minutes doing this strange dance. I had made too many mistakes. My whole life in the masjid turned into a game of how not to get hit. The mosque became my second home, my dungeon away from school, where I left my body and got lost in my imagination, silently praying to Allah that I make it out of there without getting hurt.

But the maulvis were only the first problem, and for every Mullanna Fazlur-Rehman, there was a Mullanna Muhammad who was patient, caring, and never lifted his finger against any student, a man with a refined English accent who told us stories about Jesus, Moses, Noah, and Abraham, about the well of Zamzam in Mecca, about the early battles the believers fought against the pagans, about the return of Jesus and Imam Mahdi and Dajjal—the Antichrist—in an epic showdown that was more dramatic than any movie on television. Beyond the maulvis were the older boys who attended the mosque—and they were there because their parents believed that only religion could pull them away from the streets into which they had irreversibly fallen.

These older boys were in high school and already acting like gangsters, succumbing to the violence around them. Religion—or the formal rules of religion—was their last hope. Around sunset, all the boys lined up behind the imam for the prayer and then we were let out into the darkness. That was when the real trials began, because the older boys got into scraps and brawls right outside the holy walls of Allah's house.

Ibrahim was the older brother of one of the kids in my class. He had a scar on his face, walked with a limp, bumped fists with those he liked. He had dropped out of high school for nearly killing another boy in a fistfight. Most of the boys deferred to Ibrahim, knowing that his track record on the streets was far greater than his record as a student of Islam. One of those boys who served as his disciple was Raza.

One evening a few months after starting at the mosque, my brother Oz went to the bathroom and asked me to watch over his Qur'an bag. He was in my masjid class as well, and unlike with school where we avoided each other, in the mosque we sat together. We knew that we had to stay close, for this place of worship was more dangerous than any other space we had entered. Our surroundings were unpredictable, and a fight could break out at any moment and for any reason, or no reason at all.

As our classes finished that night, I looked at the clock with liberation building in my chest.

Just ten minutes left, then I'm outta here.

I was called up to do my lesson. I got back to our spot at the same time as Oz, who let out a shriek of horror.

"My bag!" he shouted, looking around. "Where is it?"

Oz looked helpless, and I felt so foolish for taking my eyes off his bag. I knew that our father had given him a ten-dollar bill, and he had kept it safe in a bag pocket. Oz was extremely careful with money. He had been this way since he learned what money was, or perhaps from Dada's speeches about knowing the value of the dollar.

"Raza was by your bag," I whispered to Oz. "I saw him."

Oz turned to pimply Raza, who was pretending to read his Qur'an.

"You stole my money," Oz said.

Raza kept his chin on his knee, scrunched his face as though concentrating on his verses.

"I don't know what you're talking about, bro," Raza said. "You accusing me of lying?"

I heard the threat in his voice. I wanted Oz to let it go. But my brother was not me. He was unafraid of bullies and people who threatened his dignity.

"Yes, you're lying. Now turn it over, or—"

"Or what?" Raza said, smirking. "What you gonna do, pussy?"

"I . . . I'll tell my dad!"

I shook my head at my brother's innocence and knew what was coming next.

Raza said, "Watch when we get outside."

The final minutes of class that evening ticked down slowly, and my stomach was turning to water. I felt that familiar fear in my chest, in the naivete of my brother, in the violence that was coming our way.

When we were let outside, I walked at a snail's pace. I saw a small crowd gathered. There was my brother, pushed up against the bumper of the car, and Ibrahim was landing blow after blow on his shoulder. Someone was holding Oz's arm back, and all he could do was kick helplessly, shouting, "Stop it!"

And there I was, frozen like a statue, silenced and stilled by fear. Oz was crying out for help, but I could not help him. I was weak and afraid. By the time I worked up the strength to rush over to my brother, it was too late. Oz freed his arm from the kid and landed a blow to Ibrahim's chest. *My* brother, Osman, hitting them back. I was in awe of his courage, how he took a few hard punches to the body and still went after them. And I hated myself for not throwing my own body on the line. I felt the torturing thrash of shame in my skin—for I could not abide by the laws of my world that said that when they attacked two of yours, you attacked four of theirs. I could not abide by the rules of combat whereby you put your teeth and bones and knuckles before your pride and acted tough even if you were scared.

Some of the maulvis intervened and broke up the fight. Ibrahim and Raza ran away. But later that week, Oz and I would get our revenge. Hearing that the two boys wanted to jump us, we were ready when their shadows emerged from the darkness. We began hitting them with our bags and fists, blocking all their punches, emerging relatively unscathed.

The beef was dead, to be superseded by other beefs and brawls. Despite being a site of worship and religious study, the mosque was in fact a reflection of the streets outside. These older boys had been sent there to learn the way of faith, but they merely brought the code of the streets into our holy walls. Religion could not save them, save us, from the brutal reality that existed at the bottom.

By middle school, I had become adept at navigating the worlds of home, the mosque, and school—three codes of living, three modes of being, each with its own special language and rules that did not communicate to the others. By day, I was a son of the West, in my regular clothes, rapping to myself. By night, I was a Muslim, a son of the East, shape-shifting and prostrating before the One True God.

My heart—isolated, fearful, terrorized—lay somewhere in the middle.

. . .

Allah was everywhere and heard our prayers. So I prayed. I prayed to be saved from hell. I prayed for forgiveness. I prayed for big chocolate waterfalls. I prayed for unlimited wishes.

In my room, alone at night, I lay out the prayer mat with a child's fascination for the divine, imagining Allah up there in space, watching over all of us like a formless grandpa, making sure the sun rose in the morning and making sure I failed my math test on Friday. In my imagination, I was free to speak to Allah on my own terms, hoping He would hear me out, hoping He would see me.

"Dear Allah," I said one night, sitting on my prayer mat. "Please forgive me."

For some reason, I thought Allah only spoke English.

"Oh Allah," I said, shutting my eyes tighter until I imagined Him around me.

"Yes, child," came the voice.

"Are you stronger than Superman?"

"Yes," He said.

"You're bigger than the sun?"

"Yes."

"What about the moon?"

There was a silence.

"I want to be a rapper. Can you make it happen?"

"Depends," He said.

Allah was up there and I felt the connection, but then—poof!—He was gone. I would fold my prayer mat, remove my skullcap, and go to sleep with dreams of time-traveling. Then the next day, the same routine: going to school, blanking out, going to the mosque, avoiding fights, practicing my verses.

I kept up my nightly conversations with Allah for months, mumbling and whispering to God. Even though I was trying to speak to Allah, I also wanted to impress my mother. I wanted her to see that I was a religious and good child.

"Dear Allah," I said another night, "the imam says music is haram. Is it?"

There was no answer. I waited and then went to sleep.

The next night, I tried again.

"Are you mad when I skip prayer?" I asked.

I closed my eyes tighter and prayed and imagined and incanted and recited and whispered every verse I knew. I felt that I had upset Allah because I wasn't following our religion the way everyone wanted. Amma said Dada was a sinner, that the smelly black bottle I saw in his closet was "medicine." Dada said Amma was becoming a fanatic.

"I know I shouldn't fake my prayer," I said. "Sometimes my legs just get tired from going up and down. You know, Isha goes on forever. Are you mad?" I asked.

"Not really," said the voice.

"Will you send me far away?"

"Eventually."

"Far, far away, like to the moon?"

"Depends."

"On an airplane?"

"Maybe."

I held my breath. I upturned my palms. I asked, "Am I going to hell?"

There was a pause.

"Depends."

When the imam at the mosque told me there was a special prayer I could do to get a house in heaven, I ran home and stayed up all night praying. Full of enthusiasm, I threw myself at the prayer mat like an Olympic athlete.

I was on my fiftieth *rakaat* when Amma knocked on the door.

"What are you doing? You've been in here for two hours."

"I'm praying," I said.

She raised an eyebrow.

"I'm doing a *special* prayer."

"Why?"

"Because," I said, "I learned if I do this prayer, that'll make Allah happy and He'll give me a house in heaven."

I waited for her to tell me how proud she was of me.

But Amma brought her palm to her forehead in frustration. "*Tauba-Tauba*. You are sitting here past your bedtime asking for houses in paradise! That's not why we pray. Come, come, let's go, you must eat and do your homework."

I attended the mosque every evening until I was a teenager. I learned the stories of early Islam, but never learned the meaning behind those stories. The narrative passed on to me was lost in translation, filled with holes. In this case, I literally did not understand the language of these stories. What did these holy verses have to do with my life? Were my elders simply trying to pass on whatever remnants of their past selves remained? And if being Muslim was supposed to rescue me, why did I feel most ashamed about this part of my background?

As I got older, I would begin to put distance between myself and Islam, believing that if God could not save me from the boys on the street, He might not be able to save me from much worse. Religion was meant to give me purpose, a ready-made identity, but it was filtered through the interpretations of others, becoming another set of rules to get around. It took me a long time to see that Abu Bakr Masjid and the Islam that had been handed down to me were but one interpretation—that there were other stories that were not told.

But who was I when alone? Who was I when not refracting images someone else had of me? I did not know. I was lost. I wanted to feel safe. I wanted love. But all I knew were the words I had to say and the movements I had to make to hide from the world, to escape from violence, to run from shame.

4.

If God Was on That Bus

Every year, we took a family vacation: the annual Aziz summer road trip to New York. Not to New York City, but to Binghamton, upstate.

The summer of 2001 was no different. On the day of the annual adventure, Dada was under the hood of the car.

"I am giving the car a 'tune-up,'" he said.

Dada's hands were blackened and he had dark streaks around his face. He called me to stand and watch him work. "This is the battery," he said, pointing to a black box. "Don't ever leave car lights on or the battery will die. This is the transmission, that is the engine, what gives the car the power to move. This is the radiator—don't touch it or you will burn your hands. This is where the oil gauge is, use a rag to see if it's hot or it will burn your face off."

When my father finished his work, the whole family stuffed ourselves into our rickety van. We roared down the highway—Dada driving, Oz up front with a map open in his lap. Amma was in the backseat nursing my baby brother. I sat alone in the middle. Old songs rolled off our speakers, songs I did not know or appreciate, by the Rolling Stones, the Beatles, Queen, bands that my father treated as holy.

"Ra-Ra-Rasputin, Russia's greatest love machine," he sang at the top of his lungs.

As we approached the border, we came to a long line of cars stretching as far as the eye could see. Up ahead was a giant, gravity-defying sign:

UNITED STATES OF AMERICA

I sat up in my seat. Even at this young age, I felt the magnetic energy of this land to our south, this huge other country that loomed over us. Being from Canada was like sleeping next to an elephant. America was everywhere: on our TV screens, on our clothes, the music we listened to, the conversations the adults had about politics. America was like our older, wilder, richer, crazier cousin, the one who had broken free of its parents and stood proud, free, and independent.

My romantic, idealized image of America was already being born. I could feel a loosening in my chest, as though the gigantic, frenzied nation—this world beyond the barricades—was pulling me into its turmoil.

We were ten cars back. Dada fidgeted in his seat. The space inside our van suddenly grew tense, silent.

"Okay, everyone be quiet!" Dada said. "Be quiet and let me answer all the questions."

No one had said anything and no one would have thought that anyone but Dada should do the talking.

Dada squirmed in his seat again.

"Salma! Do you have the birth certificates?"

"Ji, yes," she said softly.

"Okay! Give me the documents! No one say anything. They can hear us. Our words go into the atmosphere and are recorded forever."

We were four cars back.

Up ahead, I saw a muscular white man in a dark uniform and sunglasses, gesturing for a car to go to the side.

Oz bravely asked, "Dada, why is that man pulling the car over?"

"Shhhht!" Dada said. "They are listening to us!"

"Who's listening?" I asked.

"The US government is listening! There must be a man sitting somewhere in a booth close to us who can hear everything said in the car. He could be CIA! We must be careful."

"What happens if they pull us over?" I asked.

Dada took a deep breath. "Man, oh man. They will search everything. They will take the car apart, take the seats out. They might even make us get naked and take out *pathloons* and underwear and search them. Just keep quiet now or they will hear us."

"Yes, yes," Amma replied from the back. "And they heard everything you said."

I could see that the car sent to the side was being emptied out by four officers as the family, who were Arabs, were looking on helplessly.

It was our turn. Dada drove to the stall and lowered the window. The customs agent, wearing black sunglasses, with a sharp jawline, peered into the vehicle toward me and turned his attention back to my father.

Dada removed his baseball cap. "How are you?" he asked in a friendly manner.

"Citizenship," the officer said.

"Canadian," Dada said.

"Everyone?"

"Yes, my wife also."

"Where are you going?"

"Sir, to Binghamton."

"What are you doing there?"

"Visiting family."

The agent studied our papers. I could hear my heart drumming in my ears.

"It says here you were born in . . . *Pack*-istan?"

"Yes, sir, but now I live in Canada."

"What city were you born in?"

"Sir, in Peshawar."

"And your wife?"

"She was born in Murree."

"In what?"

"Murree. M-u-r-r-e-e."

"And your children?"

"Sir?"

"The children. What are their citizenships?"

"Sir, they are also Canadian."

The agent paused, looked at Dada's face as if he were about to pull us over. I had never seen my father speaking this way. He was polite and formal.

The agent got out of the stall.

"Would you please open your trunk, sir?"

Dada froze.

"Yes, certainly, sir."

The big agent went around to the back of the car. I dared not look behind me, but I could feel the man's presence, could feel the eyes of every person in the hundreds of cars behind us, watching, guessing what this Brown family was hiding.

After a few minutes, he slammed the trunk shut. The agent came around to the driver's side. He handed Dada our documents.

"Welcome to America," he said.

"Thank you, sir," Dada said, adding, "God bless you." My father sounded relieved.

We drove through Kingston, onto the interstate, trees on either side. America was a beautiful country, and I loved staring at the scenery.

When we were safely far enough from the border, Dada said, "You see how I spoke to him, *beta*. This is how you talk to an officer of the law. The man respected me because I talked to him in a proper manner. Anytime you speak to police or a border agent, you must—*must!*—give them the utmost respect. Never talk back, because that man holds the law in his hand. If you ever break the law, I will be the first one to report you."

My father had given us this speech before. His own hand would take us before the law ever did. As a boy, I thought Dada was just being a stern and grumpy man. But as I grew older, I understood the purpose of this lecture: that if we failed to walk the tightrope of the law and made a mistake, no one was going to come and save us.

On the way to Binghamton, we drove through a small upstate town and stopped at a gas station to fill up. Dada put in gas while Amma took me and Oz into the diner to get food.

We stood at the door as Oz begged our mother to let him eat something that was not vegetarian, Amma refusing on the grounds that all meat here was haram. I looked about the room and soon realized that every single person was staring at us. Children had stopped their chattering. Men had put down their burgers. There was not a single sound in the whole diner.

My mother and brother were too busy arguing in Urdu by the cashier to notice, but I did. One of the children pointed our way, and his mother hushed him. My throat choked with shame. It was the first time that I truly felt like an alien.

But I'm just like you, I wanted to say to the children. Although I knew that something made me different, and in this corner of our continent, as in many rooms I would one day enter, difference came with judgments.

• • •

It was a beautiful September morning at the beginning of sixth grade, the sky blue for miles, the light dancing off the trees and bushes. On this ordinary day, the morning followed its usual routine—a routine that would soon be disrupted. At lunchtime, I was standing on the basketball court, happy to be starting fresh in a new grade, when suddenly my friend Dimitri ran up to me. He had brown hair and a happy personality, but he was panting, struggling to get a word out.

"What's up?" I asked.

"They closed the border!" he shouted.

"So what?" Dimitri was always telling high tales about New York and his uncles who lived there, and I thought this boy was again trying to be cool.

"You haven't heard? Two planes crashed into the World Trade Center."

I stopped dribbling. My world was so limited that I did not even know what he was talking about, so I asked, "What's the World Trade Center?"

Dimitri shoved me. I saw Shilton behind him on his purple bike, talking to some girls. The playground was full of children even younger than me.

"Stop kidding around, man," Dimitri exhorted. "This is serious. Two planes were hijacked and crashed into the Twin Towers in New York. My mom says it was terrorists . . ."

From this earnest boy's mouth, I heard that word for the first time. Only after the bell rang and we were let out of school did I understand that this might not be another exaggerated story.

When I got home, the kitchen was eerily quiet. The house felt abandoned, but the television was on. Dada was sitting at the table with a numb look on his face. Amma was next to him, and my grandmother sat by the television screen. No one said a word.

I watched their faces and saw the images on the screen: planes crashing, flames exploding, smoke billowing, towers collapsing. Dust gave rise to dust, screams to more screams, on loop, debris and chaos that felt like they had blown right into our little bungalow.

Amma looked at me and said, "*Beta*, are you ready to go to the masjid?"

I stood in cold silence, unsure of what to say, unsure why I felt that *we* were somehow connected to what was happening in New York and Washington.

"Sit down," Dada said. "You will not be going to mosque today."

He was watching the TV screen.

"Do you know what has happened?"

"Hijackings," I answered innocently.

"It is much worse. Much, much worse. This is *yu*-mungous. Every Muslim on earth is about to suffer. Pakistan will be wiped out. Listen to me. Our fellow Muslims attacked America today and killed *thousands* of people."

"Ji," Amma said. "These were not Muslims."

"Then what are they?" Dada snapped.

"They were evildoers. This is against Islam. Suicide is forbidden. Killing innocent people is forbidden. They will go straight to the hellfire."

Dada cursed in Urdu. He slammed his fist against the table. "They were *our* fellow Muslims, mine and yours. Don't you remember in Pakistan we saw people like this? They went to madrassas all day and said, 'Look at us, we are doing jihad.' Jihad, my ass. They have put every one of us in danger. They have committed a great crime. Don't you understand what's about to happen because of what these illiterates did?"

Amma sat up. Having known so much family tension, I was thrilled by the idea of skipping mosque and knew that a week of the silent treatment would follow. The look on Amma's face told me not to be happy.

Dada turned to Amma. "I am telling you right now, Salma, we will have to be careful with the children. The police will be after us."

Amma turned her mug of tea nervously. "Whatever Allah wills, we will endure it."

I kept my eyes down. I had grown used to their fighting, and like most children born into dysfunction, I learned to look away, to distance myself in my own head. But I heard everything. And in their tone I heard something I had not heard before: fear. A different kind of fear: of the state, of the state agents, of the vigilantes, of the police and the customs agents, of the terrorists.

The mosque was closed that day and the day after. As the small television rolled the footage of what would come to be called 9/11, my parents must have known that the terms of this coming war would not be ours to set. Iraq and Afghanistan would soon be bombed. The world would be at war, and people like me would have to choose: Are you with us or with the terrorists? Reality itself would be bent—no longer could there be anything as fantastical and surreally violent as commercial airliners used as missiles to bring down two of the most iconic buildings in the world. The attacks would become the lens through which I was forced to perceive the world, and the lens through which the world would perceive me.

At school, I wrote reflections and was called into the principal's office in case I "wanted to talk." But I did not want to share with anyone what I was feeling. There were children on those flights. There were mothers and fathers. There were people who had plans the next day and night. And the thought that *my* people had something to do with this filled me with guilt. In my boyish reflections, I asked, What if God was on those planes? Would He not be one of the innocents driven to their death in the name of our religion?

I could not describe the amorphous feelings of anger and heartbreak that consumed me. I did not know that Brown and Muslim and Arab people the world over would suffer the consequences of collective punishment and collective guilt. I was merely a boy who would grow up in the shadow of 9/11.

Later, on the night of 9/11, Dada called me into the other room. My brother was with me.

My father fixed his round pupils upon me and I grew scared of another beating. But this was to be a warning, a coda to all the lessons he was trying to impart.

"Listen to what I am about to tell you very closely," he intoned. "From now on, wherever you go, never discuss your religion in public. Never tell people about your background. And never reveal to the white people that you are Muslim. Do you understand me?"

We nodded. I nodded. I thought I understood.

5.

A House Divided

In the weeks after 9/11, Amma did what she could to keep life going. Dada's temper flared at random moments, and he came home from work in a rotten mood. I overheard him and Amma in the living room talking about "troubles" he was having at work. Everyone was on edge. It may or may not have had to do with the new war, but the general climate was growing more hostile for people like Dada. "Miami" became Mian again very quickly.

Later that winter, our family moved out of the bungalow and into a basement apartment. Dada said Scartown had become too dangerous and he wanted us to be closer to better high schools. He sold the house before he found a new one, so we crammed ourselves into a two-bedroom basement beneath a Polish family upstairs. At night, I lay on the floor, shivering, trying to breathe and feeling the weight of my brother sleeping next to me. Why did it always seem like my world was getting smaller?

With the move, we still attended the same school. I would return home and the words BREAKING NEWS would flash across the television screen, the broadcaster announcing that Osama bin Laden had released a new video. Bin Laden's reappearances were all people talked about. Politics entered my life in a novel way and

I felt that I was somehow implicated in the violence taking place far away from our basement.

"*Psssssssst*," Dadiye would say to me from her spot on the couch, irritated. A bald man with a smirk appeared on-screen. "What's this *kambakht* Cheney saying?"

I could not translate for her. I merely watched a parade of faces giving expert commentary on why "they" hated "us." After the attacks, the sneers and the smears bounced off the screen and into my ears, found their way echoing onto the playground, so that when the white kids said, *We see you Paki*, they spoke with a renewed authority.

Beyond the wars that would rage for two decades, a new domestic crusade was also beginning at home. It began with a phone call made to my father: the gentle closing of a door, whispers in Urdu. Mystery surrounded these private conversations. Our little home was a palace of secrets—and I trained my ears to learn what the elders were trying to keep hidden.

A couple months later, my father called me and Oz into his bedroom. He did not say much, which meant he had a lot to say but would utter just a fraction of what he was thinking.

Dada lowered his newspaper. "Your older brother is coming from Pakistan next week. We will have to make room for him."

Oz looked at me. He had these big, curious eyes that went extra oval when he was surprised. I looked back, like, *Older brother? What the— Older than me? Who?*

"We have another brother?" Oz asked.

"Yes," Dada said. "His name is Sheruu. My eldest son. You remember I told you about him?"

This was another tactic of my father's, to feign that he had already told us something when we all knew that was not the case. It was all announced like a minor logistical fact.

No further details were revealed, and I left the room having to reassess everything I took to be certain. I wondered what else I hadn't been told.

That January, we drove to the airport. The snow was falling and the highway was clear, smoky exhaust drifting up from buildings in slow motion. Negative twenty degrees. Pearson Airport was mostly empty except for the police cars lined up along the sides. I had no memories of ever being near an airport, and I watched as a few people carried their luggage and hurried to their destinations, the travelers and newcomers passing through our city.

From afar, I saw a man approach our car. He had brown skin, close-cropped hair, a light stubble. He was taller than our father, looked like he was in his midtwenties, which made him over ten years older than me.

I got out of the car and greeted him nervously.

"You're Omer," he said, pronouncing my name properly, speaking with an accent, a hint of British, a touch of Urdu. We shook hands like we were friends, and I had this wondrous feeling of recognition—my *older* brother.

He exchanged salaams with Oz and sat in the front seat. On the drive back, I noticed how awkwardly silent Dada was, making small talk, putting on his best face. When we got home, Sheruu Bhai—*bhai* for brother—said a warm hello to Amma. Sheruu called her Auntee, and Amma went out of her way to set up his room and make sure he did not miss his old country too much. The table was prepared, a brief prayer recited. It was an unusually pleasant sight, everyone calm and relaxed, and I sat and watched my older brother like he was a knight who had come to save me, save us. He had a gentle smile, ate with his hands, was immaculate in his manners, softer in his movements, so unlike our father.

I looked for any sign that Sheruu was different, foreign, exotic, but he seemed a blend of both. He said he loved cricket and he spoke perfect Urdu, but also *loved* Beyoncé and had been to places I had seen only on TV: London, New York.

Dada cleared his throat. "So, what's going on back home?"

I yawned.

"It's fine," Sheruu replied, gulping a mouthful of biryani. "With 9/11 and Afghanistan, you know, the North-West Frontier has become a war zone. Things have gotten worse but, *yaar*, life goes on."

Yaar was a word he would use often, sort of like an Urdu version of "buddy" or "homey."

"Did you hear what the Americans said?" Dada said.

"They've said a lot."

Dada leaned forward. He raised his finger. "George W. Bush told Musharraf, 'If you don't cooperate with us, we'll bomb you back to the Stone Ages.'"

Sheruu nodded in discomfort. I wondered whether he was worried about his family back home.

"Americans will do it," Dada said. "Don't doubt this Bush and this Dick. They will go to war against the whole world—Iraq, Syria, Iran, Afghanistan, Pakistan. Man oh man, it will go on for a hundred years."

Sheruu used his right hand to pick up some biryani and chicken. He burped and said, "*Shukar Alhamdulillah.*"

"Americans have been involved in Afghanistan since the 1980s," he said. "You know they funded the mujahideen to fight the Soviets . . ."

"Yes," Dada said. "That's why we have all these bloody madrassas in Pakistan now. Reagan gave hundreds of millions to Zia-ul-Haq, and Zia, that illiterate, funneled it all to extremists. You know, when I was growing up in Pakistan there was no radicalism, there was no terrorism. Only when these mullahs got their US dollars did all these problems start. Tell me, what are they saying about the attacks?"

"They don't believe the official story," Sheruu said. "That the planes were hijacked. All kinds of conspiracies they believe. The Jews did it. Bush did it."

"Dummies!" Dada said.

"Not dummies," Sheruu said. "Regular people, poor people, they don't understand how the greatest superpower in the history of the world was attacked by a man in a cave."

I listened to their conversation, wondering if I could ever know anything about politics. It went over my head, but they spoke with such passion, such *commitment*, and I sensed that the happenings of world affairs were deeply personal to them. Because, of course, they were. Toronto might be removed from the War on Terror, but Peshawar and Quetta and Islamabad and Karachi were not.

"*Chalo*," Sheruu said. "Let's see what happens."

Dada laughed to himself. He was relaxed now. He and Sheruu Bhai talked more about Pakistan, about his job prospects in Canada.

My father turned to me. "*Beta*, do you know what your older brother does?"

I shook my head.

Dada said, "He's a pilot."

I felt a rush of excitement. I couldn't wait to get to school to tell the boys.

"Yes, yes," Dada said. "He is not only a pilot, but his birthday . . ."

Sheruu gave a half-embarrassed smile and said, "I was born on September the eleventh."

...

I saw Shilton Lutchman at recess the next week. He had his durag on and a big puffy winter coat.

"Wha-gwan brejin," he said.

"I have an older brother," I said.

"Get out of here, you *rass*."

"He's a pilot. Or he's becoming one. I just met him."

"Can he rap?"

"I don't think so."

"He get the *punani*?"

"Shut up." When Sheruu Bhai picked me up from school one day, he got the nod of approval from the boys—who agreed he was very cool.

Our family life expanded after Sheruu Bhai came to live with us. Now there were seven bodies in the basement, each member of the family going about their own business, often bumping into the others outside the bathroom. There was no more room for privacy, no more space where I could be alone with my thoughts.

Amma tended to Sheruu Bhai's needs, making sure he was not lacking for anything, even though, as I later learned, Sheruu was not her son. Still, she beamed with pride, cooking his favorite dishes, making sure he felt right at home, so when he called back to Pakistan, Sheruu would report only good news. This also elevated Amma's standing in the household.

Dadiye observed Amma's newfound authority with some contempt. "Yes, yes," she said one afternoon, "I see you are becoming the big Hitler of the house."

Amma ignored her.

My older brother fascinated me. I would watch him in his room with the door slightly ajar, Bollywood music playing from the stereo as the tall, baby-faced elder stretched his legs, read through a magazine, smoked a cigarette and exhaled through his nose. His room smelled different than the other rooms, like cologne and tobacco, and he would call back to friends and laugh loudly about the colder land that was now home. This figure would become my first role model. Observing my older brother, I wondered about his life, where he had come from, how he had gotten here.

Sheruu even started working as a parking officer with Dada, father and son going to work with their thermoses, ready for the brutal winter. Late at night, I would hear him cheering in front of the television as Pakistan faced off against India in a cricket match. My attempts to get Sheruu interested in basketball and hip-hop were unsuccessful.

But the joy of his arrival was brief. Six months into living with us, a figurative bomb went off in our basement: Sheruu went to the citizenship office and legally changed his name. First name, and last. It was considered a grave matter—a matter of honor—to change one's name. Fragments of a hidden past drifted to me. As I would find out later, my older brother had a whole other identity and name in Pakistan. He had been born in Canada, I learned, but had been taken back to Pakistan at the age of one by his mother and was raised with a totally different story and name. Now he had changed his name—and to my father and grandmother, that meant disinheriting his own story.

I first heard of the name change from Dada. He was sitting at the kitchen table in his crumpled work uniform with a thermos full of chai. When I walked by him, I could tell he was seething inside, muttering to himself.

"My ex-son," he muttered. "My ex-son."

Tensions grew at home as other family members got involved in the unfolding drama. Now every day I got back from school I saw uncles and auntees sitting in our living room, fanning the flames with more rumors, whispering grievances into the elders' ears. Iqbal Mian became a regular presence, stroking his mustache, reminding my father that this dishonorable act should *never* go unpunished. To tarnish the name, the heritage, the history of our past was the greatest sin of all, Iqbal Mian said as he poured poison into our wounds.

I would walk through our door, see these strange relatives shouting or sitting in awkward silence, and go right back outside with my basketball, wandering the streets until late in the evening. Why would someone change their name? I wondered. And if they did, why was everyone so angry? I did not understand what names—with their familial histories—meant to our people. An eldest son spiting a father. Uncles and auntees spreading family discord. Prayers and gossip and intrigue, a Shakespearean drama—if the playwright was from Peshawar. To make matters worse, the name

Sheruu had adopted was Ali, meaning that my oldest and youngest brothers now had the same name. All I could do was escape into my own head.

As the arguments grew more intense, Sheruu pulled me aside.

"Get out of here or you'll rot," he said. "Go make something of yourself. Don't look back. Just get yourself out."

I didn't know what to do. Go where? Become who?

He repeated himself. "Go far away. Find a way. Go as soon as you're old enough. Don't wait."

II.

Exile Within Myself

6.

"Yung O"

Two years after the Twin Towers fell, our family moved out of the basement and into a house on the other side of the city.

We packed our things and departed for the western frontier of Toronto, to a city called Mississauga. After two years of living in the basement, it all happened as if overnight. Dada had purchased a house in the suburbs, and we up and moved. I was in the middle of eighth grade, and the decision was made without explanation. Because nothing was communicated in our family, it was expected that I simply adjust to a new world without complaint or issue. Quietly, I grieved the loss of friends and the familiar sidewalks.

One final day in Scartown, I said goodbye to Shilton. He was sitting on his purple bike, riding around in the cold like we did, and I saw those curious eyes and that cool smile. His headphones were above his ears, and he'd been playing me some tracks he had recorded, singing the hooks and dropping his own bars.

"You leavin' deh Lutchman?" he asked.

"I don't want to," I said.

The sunset behind him was a blazing pink, creeping behind dark apartment buildings. Shilton extended his fist and I bumped it back. "Don't forget about me," he said. "When I make it as an

R&B star, I'll come find you." We laughed, but later, as Scartown disappeared in my rearview, I wondered when I might see him again.

• • •

This journey from the basement to a two-story home was being made by immigrants all over the city. At last, the great North American dream: a house of one's own, a mortgage and a front yard, neighbors and manicured roads of that great, isolating wilderness known as the suburbs.

The house was bigger, and now I had my own room. Our first night in the new city brought a snowstorm. It was icy out and mounds of snow filled the driveway. The house even had a fireplace, rusty, unused. Because the heater was not working, my father decided we would try to warm ourselves the old-fashioned way.

"Let's go get firewood," Dada said.

My brother and I hopped in the car and rode to the hardware store. The snow had settled, lights reflecting off the shiny asphalt. We pulled into a parking lot, but Dada drove right past the store and stopped next to a dumpster.

"Come on, help me get the *lakri*."

I followed my father behind the green waste container and we scavenged around for wood, stacking up logs that were not logs but had splinters and needles poking out, some with grease slathered on the outside. I cut my thumb, though I did not tell my father, fearful of his temper. In the distance, I saw the hardware store, bright Christmas trees, boys and girls talking happily with their parents as they came out of the store with a light glow, and I felt the pinprick of loneliness.

"They raised the price," Dada said at home to my mother, who questioned why we had gotten this moldy, splintered wood. "Be grateful we even have a place to live. If it wasn't for my hard work, you and your whole family would still be in Pakistan."

She ignored him. We stood around the fireplace and watched Dada light the wood.

"This will not work," Amma said.

Dada lit a paper towel and tossed it inside the charred, dirty little fireplace. He checked to make sure the fireplace's flue was open. The embers crackled around the wood, the wood turned orange, the smoke rose.

"See! See!" Dada said, happy that we would warm ourselves and save money in the process.

But the smoke kept growing thicker, darker, and the alarm rang in the house. Soon, black fumes rose out of the fireplace, spreading through the living room and kitchen, choking up our lungs.

"Quickly, outside!" Dada shouted.

He panicked and began putting out the fire. I ran outside in my pajamas, shivering in the cold, my mother and grandmother following behind me. Sirens blared nearby; the fire truck on its way. I looked down the line of houses and wondered why, despite this new house, we still felt poor.

For over an hour, I watched from the snowy sidewalk as the firefighters did their work. The whole evening was a comedy of errors.

That night, and for many nights throughout the winter, I slept wearing three sweaters and two pairs of socks, trembling in my bed. It was not just the burnt stench of wood or the dry cold that kept me awake, but the fact that I felt so alone that not even my imagination could save me. I was now in a new town, nameless and faceless, wondering whether the house fire was not an omen for the trials ahead.

• • •

Everyone in the household adjusted to the new city in their own way. Dada worked long hours. Oz and I went to school and did the extra chores our father gave us. Amma took a part-time job at a gas station because money was tight. I would see her come home from work, yellow and red shirt on, silver name tag that read SALMA. Amma donated a portion of her paycheck to charity every month, even when she had little money. Dadiye learned the sidewalk routes and walked the neighborhood with me.

Families of all colors lived in Mississauga, especially Chinese, Pakistanis, Indians, Trinidadians, and Palestinians. The houses were physically close, but there was an emotional distance. We all lived in vastly different and well-guarded worlds.

• • •

When I got to Rick Hansen Secondary School in 2004, I stumbled upon a brave new world. The school was a fortress containing two thousand bodies. Everyone was divided along ethnic lines, Afghans hanging with the Afghans, Vietnamese with the Vietnamese. Different parts of the school were reserved for certain groups: the Black bench only for Black kids, the atrium for the Punjabis. Unlike in Scartown, where I hid my ethnic background, here the boys proudly burnished their heritages. Their flags hung out of

their jeans or backpacks and if they weren't repping their nation-
alities, they had the blue or red bandanas of the Bloods or Crips,
markers of individual and collective strength. The makeup of the
school could be discerned by the names of the cliques that roamed
together: Tamil Tigers, Brown Assassinz, Hot Boyz, AraB Thugz.

Outside by the Smoker's Pit, at the edge of school property,
I saw the Brown kids smoking spliffs and puffing on cigarettes,
twelfth graders, dropouts, expellees, older boys promising pretty
girls a ride in their souped-up cars. The gap between parents and
children was too great, and most parents, like my own, had no clue
of what was going on outside their doors. I sensed that these boys
were as lost as me and I might end up where they were, without any
hope of advancing beyond the limited climax reached at eighteen.

In this school, which felt to me like a prison, I was a lone traveler, keeping to myself, shy and afraid of messing with the wrong
person. I was friendless and cousinless in a place where being either
made you a target.

"Yo, clown," one of the older students said to me in the hallway. "Throw this out for me." He handed me his garbage. I did not
know that this was a test of honor and I was supposed to refuse
and face the consequences. Innocent and averse to conflict, I took
his garbage and walked it over to the trash.

Occasionally, I took out a red notebook I had been writing in
for a number of years, jotting down poems and ideas. I had to be
careful no one caught me, but one of the boys—bandana, Pakistani
flag—saw me writing in it and asked what I was doing.

"Nothing," I said, terrified.

"Let me see that."

He snatched the notebook out of my hands and read it aloud so that students walking by would hear. They laughed out loud as he tossed my notebook back at me.

"You writing poetry? What are you, a faggot?"

I went red with shame. One of the white girls I had a crush on, a brunette named Nina, overheard. I thought she was going to tell the boy off, but she walked up to me, inspected my sullen gaze, and asked the first boy, "Who's this crusty kid?"

They laughed. I wandered the halls wishing I could be anyone else. I went to the bathroom and looked at my face, at my round glasses, at my cheeks and the peach fuzz on my chin, hating everyone around me. I pressed my fingers against my skin and wondered, *What is so crusty about me?*

I saw no purpose to the classroom any longer. Quadratic equations? Lance has a shank in his locker. *A Midsummer Night's Dream?* Suleiman ran over a boy in his car. The composition of atoms? Stephen had pulled out a handgun during a fistfight.

In survival mode, I began to assemble my latest mask. I had to shed my softness. My jeans got baggier. My haircut got more faded. I began to carry myself with a particular gait that signaled authority, communicating I would not back down. Inside, I was deeply afraid. I was afraid the way all these boys who brawled and battled and fought were afraid. Some had lived through real wars in their old lands; violence was all they knew. Others merely wanted to be seen as heroes, to claim some limited glory for themselves, because we had no other heroes around us. The whole pose of strength was an elaborate facade, but one that was required by the jungle—and one that I very quickly adopted, made my own.

...

It was in the hallways of tenth grade that one of the boys christened me with a new nickname.

"What's cracking, Yung O?" he said. The name stuck, the first word inevitably misspelled, and I began to adjust to the tough demeanor that was expected of the moniker. I adopted the code of these hallways and soon linked up with a crew that participated in regular fights. These weren't fair battles, but all-out brawls, with ten or twenty or thirty kids going to war, even if it was against a single person who'd then call their cousins for help.

This was how I got into my first beef. It was against a boy named Jamie, a biracial boy who had curly hair and a high-pitched voice and was always kind to me, even buying me fries when I forgot my lunch. But by the strictures of these hallways, I had to fight him, since a rumor had started that Jamie had insulted my mother. I knew it was not true, but that did not matter.

"You gotta scrap him," said a boy from my crew. "Back of the school. Don't be a pussy."

I wished I could have said no. I did not like to fight, but now my persona demanded it.

Me and Jamie faced off in the fields after school one October evening. There were only four or five boys there, forming a semi-circle around us. A rap song played loudly off somebody's flip phone, a track called "City Is Mine" by an up-and-coming local MC named Drake.

I squared up, fists ready, eyes steady. Jamie threw a punch right at my face. I saw double, blinked, saw triple, blinked, and landed my knuckles against his jaw. He threw multiple blows and struck my cheek. My teeth rattled and my brain shook. I spat blood in my hands. My shirt was stained red.

After the fight ended, we all parted ways. The boys got their entertainment, and I got myself involved in a senseless act of violence. I limped home alone, spitting blood the entire way. *What a dumb person you are*, I cursed to myself. *Fighting someone you don't even want to fight.*

· · ·

During the school year, my grades dipped lower than the temperature. Some of my teachers tried to help. I was secretly interested in a few of their lessons, but I could not show it. History was the subject that aroused my curiosity, though I sat in the back of the class, slumped in my chair, doodling and acting out my apathy.

My English teacher, Miss T., who liked to chug her two-gallon bottle of water in the middle of her sentences, assigned us a book called *Lord of the Flies*. It was about a group of schoolchildren who had landed on an island and slowly turned into barbarians. Reading the novel, I imagined that all of us boys in Sauga were like the kids in the story, isolated on our suburban island away from the cities, away from the museums, away from our parents, descending into pits of anarchy.

One day after class, Miss T. pulled me aside. She looked at me like a fallen son who, if she did not help now, would forever be stuck in the cycles she saw around her.

"Omer," she said, "I read your paper. It wasn't bad, but you can make it better by working a little harder. You have *potential.*"

I glanced at her face for any sign of deception, as though part of me was certain that she was lying.

"Yes, you have potential. But you have to work, build your vocabulary. You know, you could be a teacher one day, or a lawyer, but you can't do anything if you don't try."

I shrugged, but part of me did not believe her.

That evening after school, I ditched the boys and wandered into our small library. Half the books in the school were worn-out from overuse and the other half looked brand-new, like they had never been touched. I was watching over my shoulder in case anyone saw me there, ducking into one of the stacks when a group of girls passed.

My eyes darted over the spines. There was so much to know. I pulled out a book by a man I had never heard of. He had a hand-some face, big glasses, a fierce look in his eyes.

The Autobiography of Malcolm X, said the title. He was Muslim, which made me want to know what he had to say. I checked out the book and went upstairs to one of the many stairwells where no one would find me. I opened the book like it was contraband and started to read, tracing each word with my finger.

"When my mother was pregnant with me, she told me later, a party of hooded Ku Klux Klan riders galloped up to our home in Omaha, Nebraska, one night."

I was struck by the force of his words. As I read, I began to lose myself, deciphering each page like it contained hieroglyphics. The story captivated my under-stimulated brain and I wanted to know more, thrilled by this little secret of reading when no one was around.

"What are you doing?" said a voice.

I looked up in terror. It was Sujit, one of the toughest boys in the school. I held the book behind my back.

"Uh . . . nothing," I stammered. "Just here, you know, chilling."

"You reading? What you doin' with that?"

"Nah, nah, this is nothing," I said, gripping the hardcover. "Just an assignment."

"Let's go run ball, g."

I slipped the book in my bag and went to go play basketball. Soon enough, I was pulled right back into the culture around me. When the book was due back at the library, I returned it without finishing it. While my curiosity of the larger world had been awakened, it was in conflict with my understanding of the realities before my eyes. I had internalized somewhere deep that reading and learning were for *other* people. I was young and I was naive. I did not know myself, nor did any of the immigrant and first-generation kids around me. No common narrative bound us together. I was lost. We were lost. Aimless, rootless, without our own history, quickly going astray—and with no one to save us.

7.

Honor Code

After I became more of a goon, I finally started getting noticed by the girls at school. Soon enough I was involved with a young West Indian girl named Erica. She was petite with a dark complexion and spoke half her sentences in English and the other half in patois. The first week I knew her, I whispered, "I love you."

Erica looked at me in shock and laughed to herself. "You don't know what those words mean."

We held hands in the hallways and I had my first kiss. Finally! A girlfriend! Together, Erica and I skipped classes and went to the mall. We hung out after school until it got dark. I met her whole family, her father barbecuing the best spicy chicken I had ever tasted. Until then, I had disliked the most basic qualities about myself: too brown, too short, too shy, too ugly. Erica made me feel worthy of love.

But I was unprepared for the norms of relationships and sex. My father's only advice about girls, spoken in passing, was "Don't get emotionally involved." What he meant was that to be emotionally attached was dangerous, volatile. I knew his relationship advice was not to be taken seriously. After his first divorce, he never entirely trusted women.

Dada said, "The woman you marry, make sure she does a blood test and an IQ test, otherwise you will be unhappy."

Thanks, I thought.

Meanwhile, my grandmother warned me about white women in particular. She believed that the *goris* would steal my heart and corrupt my mind, just like these freedom-bearing, liberated women had broken the heart of her older brother, the doctor, after he fell madly in love with a white nurse in London decades ago and gave her all his possessions.

"Keep yourself protected," Dadiye warned. She meant: don't give your heart away to just anybody.

Amma had a similar idea about love. For her, any relationship before marriage was illicit, haram. Our rules around sex were strict, and some of the teenagers around me would soon grow up to have their own arranged marriages. Love was complicated enough before the elders got involved, and when they were informed about a relationship, it was because marriage had entered the equation. So I kept my infatuation a secret. I walked home with Erica and parted ways when my house was in sight. When Erica picked me up in her car, I asked that she not park outside my house but down the street. Little compromises like these allowed me to keep my home life and love life fully segregated. With my parents, I followed the unspoken rule of *Don't ask, don't tell.*

Nor was I the only one keeping this world of boyfriends and girlfriends hidden. Most other kids at school did the same. Some of the Muslim girls would change out of their more conservative clothes when they got to school, their stern fathers having no idea that their daughters had fallen for a boy. One girl in my class was seen with her boyfriend and was quickly pulled out of school and married to an older man in Pakistan. For the girls, the consequences of being found out could be dire.

I felt like a hypocrite every time I walked into my house, guilt constricting my throat. I told Erica she could not meet my parents, lying that it had to do with their busy work schedules. I lied to my parents about not having a girlfriend and lied to myself about why I was lying to everyone. Any action on my part would disappoint or offend someone close to me: be open about my relationship and Amma would say I was sinning; be honest with Erica about my traditions and I would deeply hurt her feelings.

The double life took a toll. I began having headaches in the middle of the night, waking up out of breath, the anxiety like a stone on my chest. Focusing on impurity, my culture turned me into a practiced perjurer: wanting to love, wanting to *be* loved, but always holding part of myself back.

In our customs, a man would grow up, have a career, and then marry a woman of a similar background. In the past, the marriage would be arranged, although today one's parents still played an important role in selecting partners. My own parents had only met on their wedding day. Love was shrouded in silence, suffocating silence, suffering silence. The Talk did not exist in our household, or any household I knew. The Talk was forbidden, like eating pork. Those two words—"The Sex"—were banned. In fact, Amma was so terrified that I would get a girl pregnant that she told me she prayed every day that I did not commit a *ghalat kham*—literally, a "terrible act." Nor did school help. Sex Ed was just anatomy and abstinence, without any lessons about emotions, trust, intimacy, vulnerability, honesty. I had to learn how to be with women the hard way: by going through heartbreaks in silence.

One day when I was sixteen, I got home from school and saw Amma having a panic attack. She was sweating, talking to herself, walking up and down the stairs. My heart began to race and I felt, not for the last time, that I was guilty of a grave crime. In a split second, I remembered that Erica had made a little box of photographs for me that I hid in the closet. My mother must have discovered them while cleaning. The blood drained from my face. I was right.

"Let's go," Amma said. She took my arm and rushed me into the car and we drove with urgency, running a red light. I was terrified. The photos were not R-rated—they featured Erica and me hanging out, although there was one where we were kissing.

Amma parked right outside the mosque. From her purse, she took out a Qur'an.

"Do not commit *zina*," she said. This was the Arabic word for sexual intercourse before marriage.

"What?" I said. "This is crazy."

"Swear on this."

"For what?"

She made me put my hand on the Qur'an.

"Swear that you will not do *zina* and have kids before marriage."

"This is stupid," I said.

"Say you will not get a girl pregnant before marriage!"

"Okay," I said, wanting this embarrassing ordeal to be over. "I won't."

"And swear you will break things off with this girl."

I removed my hand from the Qur'an. "No, that's for me to decide."

Amma pointed a finger in my face. "No kids before marriage."

The inquisition lasted less than ten minutes. We drove home in silence, the most awkward minutes of my young life. Amma saw a future for me that terrified her: fathering children in high school; dropping out; bringing disrepute to the rest of the family. She had been conditioned by our culture to assume the worst when it came to relationships.

But because I was a boy, I had it easy. I realized that if the feeling of a pressure-cooker home forced me to conceal myself, then the women in my community had it ten times worse. They had to face not just the sexism of the outside world but the limiting beliefs of their families, especially conservative clans who saw freedom as a threat and liberation as cultural suicide. Women were to know their place, and they rebelled daily against the rules placed on them by their families. This was not even about religion, since many girls who wore the hijab were on their way to becoming doctors, scientists, lawyers, choosing their own partners. It was about a conservative, tribal, feudal outlook that twisted into codes of honor. Violating these codes could get women killed.

There was a girl who lived down the street from me, a girl I never met but whose story seared itself in my mind. Her name was Aqsa Parvez. Her parents had immigrated from Pakistan. Like a lot of young women, Aqsa was a rebel, wearing Western clothes, texting boys, discovering her own femininity. I saw the headline in the newspaper the day she was murdered. Aqsa's brother, with her father's approval, strangled her to death in their home. Aqsa's decision to live a normal life was seen as a threat and insult to the honor of her family. For that, she was to be summarily executed by the men who were supposed to protect her.

Reading her story, I felt anger at the men of our community. Who would do something so extreme to keep their daughters and sisters from being happy? Had our minds become so poisoned by the fear of sexual freedom that we could end the life of a woman simply because she dared to be herself? Why did we trap our daughters into cycles of violence rather than uplifting them?

Even though my parents were aghast at the murder in our neighborhood, I overheard one distant uncle say under his breath, "Why did she have to dress like that?" He got a loud rebuke from my father. I clenched my fists, shook my head, and walked away, aware that I lacked the vocabulary in Urdu to articulate my disgust.

Aqsa came to mind often, how her life had been cut short because of the toxic imaginations of the men around her. Brown women were the real freedom fighters. They were waging covert wars, clandestine operations for liberty, blazing their own paths against the shameful culture of sexism that existed outside their doors, and the shameless misogyny that existed behind them.

Honor, dishonor, shame, *sharam*: the roots of violence.

• • •

Around the time I entered tenth grade, Sheruu Bhai decided to return to Pakistan. He had lived with us for just four years. Now he would leave.

When I saw my older brother downstairs flipping channels in his sweatpants and *chuppal*, switching between CNN and basketball— he had, at last, become a fan—I was desperate to know why he was moving.

"*Yaar*," he said, "the time has come."

"What do you mean? You can be a pilot here, can't you?"

He gave a long sigh. "It's difficult now, you know. The war, the licensing issues. I could stay. But sometimes, we just have to go home."

I waited for him to give me the real answer. He looked at me and said, "One day you'll understand."

That was a phrase both he and my father used: *One day you'll understand.* When other explanations did not suffice, the elders resorted to this age-old expression.

I made a face. I grumbled. I wanted him to stay.

"Listen, yaar," he said. "This place is not everything. Our homes can pull us in and keep us stuck. There is a big world out there. Go explore it. Make something of yourself. Don't let your life go to waste."

"How?" I asked.

"Dude," he said, glowering with big eyes. "You were born in the Western world. You can do anything."

"Why can't you stay?"

He sighed again. "Pakistan is where my roots are."

A few weeks later, I said goodbye to my older brother. I felt like I was only getting to know him, like he had just gotten off that plane. Now he was leaving for good.

I went to shake his hand at the door. He pulled me in for a hug and kissed my head.

"You take care of yourself, all right?"

When he left, I returned to my room, thinking about the advice he had given me. The house felt emptier than the day we moved in.

8.

War

A nger was brewing in my heart. I would sit in my classes and doodle in my notebook, ears alert to the consuming beefs around me. I began acting out at school, getting in trouble, getting suspended. When my guidance counselor called me in for "a chat," I sat down across from the man with his goatee, slumped in my chair, indifference on my face.

"So, what do you want to do with your life?" he asked.

"I don't know," I said. "Maybe the warehouse."

The guidance counselor nodded as if he'd gotten me to state my career path without trying.

What I thought was: I skipped school yesterday and got drunk with my friends and had the spins so bad that I puked into a trash can and felt guilty all evening for violating my religion. Joey offered me a spliff and I turned it down only because I would get a beating if my father found out I was high. The boys passed around benzos and other pills, but I was too scared of what they'd do to me. I've missed so much class that the principal threatened me with suspension and said I would never be able to take university-level courses. He said I could kiss any chances of an academic path goodbye. *Listen up,* I wanted to ask him, *what's your education supposed to help me with?*

At home, when my father saw my report card, he was apoplectic. He shook his head furiously.

"Doctor or engineer you must become!" He was red in the face. "You're turning into a flunky, a failure," he said. "You're going to be homeless, then see if any of your friends take you in. You think you're a big tough guy now, but the world is going to spit you out like you're nothing."

Flunky, fluke, failure. I accepted that I was mediocre, and I thought: *Fuck school.*

On a balmy June day, the teacher walked into history class with a police officer in tow. The teacher was a heavy woman with blond hair who was instructing us about World War II, Mussolini, Hitler, the liberation of Europe, the heroic efforts of soldiers and peacemakers.

"Settle down, everyone," she said. "Today we have something important to talk about. . . ."

I closed my notebook with the doodles. The police officer had a shaved head. He stood by the whiteboard, staring out at us.

The officer cleared his throat. Since the fights at school had become so frequent, cops were regularly seen in the hallways. They were at the doors, they were by the gym, they were near the Smoker's Pit. Expulsions had gone up. You had to snitch on your friends if you knew some information the principal or police could use.

"Ahem," the officer said. "I don't know if you guys read the news this morning. Federal police in Mississauga have arrested eighteen men on charges of terrorism. Some of the alleged terrorists were your age."

The cop took a step forward. He stood with his legs wide apart, and even the tough boys at the back stopped their murmurings.

"What I'll say is, if any of you know the suspects or interacted with them in a social capacity, don't hesitate to come forward and talk to us. As your teacher said, some of these suspected terrorists were from this very neighborhood and went to schools nearby." He paused for a moment. The class was quiet.

"*Snitches*," the boy next to me coughed.

The cop left.

Our teacher sighed. "Turn your textbooks to page 319. We'll be learning about Adolph Hitler today."

I had become so indifferent to the happenings around me that the news did not fully register until I was in the hallways and everyone was chatting about this announcement. A newspaper was passed around, girls and boys noting how so-and-so was a friend of so-and-so and they never thought he would do this. The story was worse than I had imagined. The boys, the youngest close to my age and most of them in their late teens and early twenties, had planned to bomb Parliament. They wanted to create an al-Qaeda cell in Toronto. They sought to shoot up mass crowds, take hostages, storm Parliament, behead the prime minister. They had tried to buy a powerful fertilizer used in the making of bombs, but the person on the other end of the sale was an undercover federal agent.

Soon enough, my suburb was on CNN and Fox News. The angry youth were labeled the Toronto 18. I saw even more police in our neighborhood. My brother was stopped and questioned on his way home, asked by a man in black clothes—who we assumed was an undercover fed—where he was going.

At home, the fuse was lit.

"See this," Dada said, rushing into the kitchen with the newspaper and throwing it on the table. "The jihadis have come here!" He began pacing back and forth, rambling, pulling on his hair. "They will come for us! The FBI, RCMP, CIA, MI6 will be outside our door. I have seen a van sitting outside. They will tap our phones. They will be in the mosque."

Amma read the news story. Calmly, she said, "We cannot live in fear."

Dada had gone red in the face. "They should all be *hanged*."

"If they are found guilty," Amma said, "they will receive the correct punishments."

"No, Salma, you don't understand. They were brainwashed by mullahs. Do you ever notice that it's young men the recruiters send to kill us all?"

I listened, but I could not make sense of what these young men had tried to do. Here I was, suppressing every bit of my Muslim identity, paying my religion no attention, and there were these men in my community who wanted to kill others in the name of Islam. They could have been my cousins.

Chaos began to engulf me. I felt my anger like a second pulse in my veins; anger toward my father for his worship of grades and the law; anger toward my mother for her unceasing devotion to religion; anger at my teachers for not understanding my struggles. This anger was contaminating every facet of my life, just as the rage of these young men had corrupted their minds. The difference between us was that I had spent every evening of my youth in the masjid with the maulvis, receiving an Islamic education, and this had inoculated me from any temptation toward radicalism. There was no glamor in religion for me.

Yet as I grew older, the narrative of these men and their brethren in other suburbs in America and Europe who would seek to conduct similar acts of criminal violence was demystified. The young men had dreamt up a fantastical plot that transformed a video game brutality into real life. For once, they were to become heroes of their own stories, protagonists seeking vengeance on behalf of Muslims they would never know. Mimicking the glory of conquerors, they had replaced our meaningless reality with a life of purpose; distorted, disfigured, but one where God would reward them for mass murder. Islam had been repurposed in their vacant minds as a creed of holy war, a pathway to eternal liberation, and this in turn would elevate them and they would transcend the daily drudgeries of nothingness that our world laid out for us. Why be just another aimless immigrant son when you could be a holy warrior?

I quietly asked myself what sort of reality these boys had been living. The answer came later: they had been living mine.

• • •

It was as though a gust of medieval wind had blown in from the desert and swept away the old, private Islam with a muscular, political alternative.

Life grew more turbulent at home. My father threatened divorce, *talaq*, which hung over our house like a dark cloud crackling with thunder. Religion. Domestic turmoil. Relationship thorns. Amma told me that when I was younger, I would cry and say, "I don't like divorce." Now as a teenager, I didn't say anything.

Amma was growing obsessive about Islam, trying to impose it on me. I was beginning to resent her, to resent my father, my whole family. We were coming apart as a family, a house divided against itself. I wondered later if every immigrant family was secretly unhappy, aware that theirs was a transient existence, aware that the kids would either justify the parents' sacrifices or be punished for them.

Around this time, Amma quit her job at the gas station and began attending an Islamic institute for women. Middle-class and working-class auntees gathered together, drank chai, discussed the transliterations of the Qur'an. Many of the women had gone through rough times and had turned to Allah for sustenance. The love that was to come from family life and marriage was replaced by the love of God.

One day when I returned home, pulling up my jeans, tucking in my shirt, I saw Amma with a new black scarf over her head. Usually, she covered her head with a bright dupatta like the other auntees.

"Do you like it?" she said, flashing a joyful smile, the first I had seen in a long time.

"Ji, Amma," I said respectfully.

"I have decided to wear the hijab," she said.

I did not ask her why, but she quickly added, "It is a personal decision I have made for my Maker. Your father might not like it, but I do this for my faith. . . ."

My body went tense, my instinctive shame numbing my limbs. It brought me no pleasure knowing that I saw my mother's hijab as another mark of difference.

Over the next months, Amma became a kind of nun, dispensing religious advice at all hours. Her weekly attendance at the institute soon turned daily and she devoted herself to understanding the meaning of the Qur'an, word for word, verse for verse. I imagine Amma's existence was lonely and this sisterhood of the faithful gave her a community outside of our turbulent family.

Amma's new spiritual journey began to manifest itself in other ways. In the car, she would turn off our rap songs and play Qur'an recitations. She shared the lessons her female teacher, whom they called Ustaad, passed on to them, about a woman's duties to her family, her children, her work, her community. Dada was paranoid, thinking these women were trying to spread fundamentalist Islam—and conquer their husbands in the process.

"She is Wahhabi," Dada said. "She wants us to go backwards."

"No," Amma retorted, "I want us to move forward in our faith."

The battle lines were sharpened. Amma's rebirth into Islam meant that the gulf between us widened. In later years, I saw how Amma's faith had guided her through a difficult marriage, through a new country where she had to learn new customs, a new language, all the trials of being a Muslim woman in a world that told her she was nothing more than an oppressed victim of religion. Her scars were written on her face, in the dark circles deepening under her eyes.

But I did not wish to take the same spiritual journey. I had begun to lose my faith and saw no path of redemption. God was neither on this bus nor in my heart; God had disappeared from my life, and every time He was mentioned, it was because another bomb had gone off and fingers were pointed in the direction of my people. Nor was the US War on Terror in the front of my mind. Other battles were scorching our community. Amma was praying intensely one night after she returned from the Islamic Institute. A sister at the mosque had been weeping and nearly passed out. Her son had been murdered the night before, the latest casualty of our neighborhood hostilities. The boy, just sixteen, had been shot outside the theater over a beef that amounted to "Yo, you looking at me?" That was all it took, as though by being seen, one's shame, and therefore one's rage, had been exposed. Bodies piled up in this way—and they did not make headlines for longer than an hour. I thought of the boy's final moments, of countless other boys. A wordless tragedy: after one's parents had struggled to set up a new life—to then die on a summer night, in a half-empty parking lot of a suburban theater.

War was everywhere now: in Afghanistan, in Iraq, in Palestine, in New York and Washington and London and Toronto. War had come to my neighborhood, tearing apart families and neighbors, as the police agents descended into our community. The war resided in my own heart, and I was succumbing to my rage.

I was dangerously lost, gravitating toward the streets—the streets with their magnetic pull and offer of kinship. Lost, like the boys around me; lost in my own suffocating unreality. This was my world, quivering on its axis, tipping toward anarchy as time ticked away.

9.

Revelation

I never really believed in miracles, not since I was little. Life was what it was; you either adjusted or were trampled underneath the stampede of events. More of the same was likelier than a sudden shift in perception. That was what I had come to accept. Miracles only happened in the movies.

The last year of high school was definitive in Canada, the moment when students were parceled out onto their different paths, college or university for some, manual labor and the service industry for the rest. Adulthood was pressing itself upon me, but I was so far behind that the thought of trying to catch up left me exhausted.

"You will go to university," Dada said. "You *must* go to university." He had the immigrant's mindset that higher education would allow me to escape the trap that had devoured his own life: dropping out to feed his family, sending his wages back to Pakistan, helping his relatives escape poverty in Pakistan or try to immigrate to the West, and never fulfilling his full potential.

My grandmother whispered to me, "Get scholarship, get scholarship." I didn't think she even knew what a scholarship was or how difficult it was to obtain, but even if she did, my grades were too low.

Amma echoed these sentiments. "I pray that you do something with your life and not just end up worse than us when we came to Canada."

Why don't you *go to university*, I wanted to tell them, with all the attitude of an arrogant teenager. Both my parents had attended college in Pakistan, but had abruptly left their studies behind. They did not go to elite schools or private academies where, I would later learn, the top echelons of Pakistani society sent their kids, to be shuttled off later to America and England. They went to public institutions, but were forced to abandon dreams of further study because life demanded migration and wages to be earned for survival. University came to represent the way out. University was the path to a stable career, a job worth having, some semblance of progress. And I was the oldest of their kids born in the West: If I did nothing, what example would this set? Higher education thus symbolized a kind of liberation, a mountaintop that no one in the family had yet reached.

I had always been a curious boy, but nothing was more outlandish in my environment than pursuing my own academic interests. Everyone around me at school frowned upon academic excellence—and I had come to accept, with alarming ease, that I was simply a dumb kid, a fuckup who would not even surpass the low bar that his teachers, friends, community had set for him.

The wider world was alien to me. I saw no one in my neighborhood who I might emulate, saw no role models I wished to follow. I had never stepped foot outside the suburbs, unless it was to Binghamton. I did not know how to apply myself, did not have a "why" for which to live.

My not-caring attitude protected me. If I had given school my best shot and still done poorly, the judgments of the school and my family would have been confirmed. There could be no motivation where there was no purpose.

I needed some kind of intervention, a sign, a signal to imagine an alternative future for myself. And that was when I saw him.

. . .

That September, after turning seventeen, I got home from school early and walked to the living room to check on Dadiye and what she was doing.

My grandmother was sitting at her usual spot on the couch, sipping chai and watching the news. She switched the channel from her daytime television shows of Oprah and Dr. Phil and put on CNN. I wolfed down some biryani, ready to ignore whatever bin Laden mixtape had just dropped and the endless analysis of its contents.

But there was someone else on the screen. He was tall with an angular frame, dark brown skin, a deep voice, talking about his father's journey to America, a country where all things were possible.

I stopped chewing.

"Who's that?" I asked Dadiye in Urdu.

Dadiye glanced from the television to me. "That is Barack Obama. He is standing up for president of the United States. His full name is . . . Barack *Hussein* Obama."

I stood, stunned, solitary in my amazement. It wasn't just how the man looked but what he was saying: how his name had given him problems, how he had struggled to see a place for himself in the world, how one's background should not be a barrier to one's success, how he was running for the highest office in the land to help those who had been left behind.

I could have left it at that, ignored his words, stepped outside into the dry, airless evening, back to the emptiness of my world. But something told me to stop and pay attention.

"Hussein?" I said. "Obama?" I felt a hint of recognition. There was nothing funny about his name. *Barkat* meant "blessing" in Urdu, and every third person around me could have been named *Hussein*. The name *Obama* might sound dangerous to people who had never heard these letters together, but I knew a kid named Osama and he was one of the nicest boys at school and one of the best basketball players. The man on the screen could have been any of my kin. No, he was not foreign at all.

I watched how he spoke, his elegant demeanor, the way he walked and took up space, each one of his movements challenging my every assumption about people.

After the news moved to the next story, I rushed to the phone and called my father, asking for permission to use our computer. The desktop was still a treasured piece of technology in 2007, and I had no cell phone or any other communication device. I sat in front of the computer and read every article I could find about the man. I learned that his grandfather was a Muslim, that his forefathers had been colonized by the British, that he always had trouble with how he looked. Then I watched his speech at the 2004 Democratic National Convention, startled by the story he told. I played it on loop, six times in a row, his words hitting me like thunderbolts to the skull: the immigrant father, the feeling of being stuck between worlds, the search for roots, the need to connect to something outside himself.

For hours, I read everything about this man called Obama, his education, his rise to Harvard Law School. Even *I* knew what Harvard was, some fabled place from the movies. Through Obama's biography, I looked up the books he read, what he studied in university. Never before had I seen a man who resembled someone from my community speaking with such eloquence and purpose. The range of my horizons expanded infinitely in that moment. Obama spoke of America as a land where all dreams were possible, a tolerant country where your name was not a barrier to your success. He made studying and reading seem *cool*. Obama was the opposite of every man I had known until then, and I felt he was speaking directly to me, not lecturing or hectoring, but gently showing me that I could be more than my surroundings.

I jumped up off the chair. *Could I become a lawyer? Could I go to one of the top schools in America?* My instinct was to say, "Never," but then there was this skinny man with the funny name in front of me, standing up for the highest office in the world. He seemed to be saying, *If you work hard and have hope, you can do anything.*

Academic study, once a grim endeavor, suddenly became important. I didn't know what a GPA or SAT was, but by the time I was done at the computer, it was night outside and I was shivering with nervous energy.

Obama showed me that books and knowledge were not for other people and that I could educate myself out of my apathy. Seeing him made me yearn for a different kind of life, one of learning and politics, a life of exploration and action. It was as though a circuit of two previously disconnected wires were brought together in my head, creating fireworks in my neurons. For the first time, I believed I had agency in choosing a new life. For the first time, I was aware that I could become someone else, a by-product of my imagination and not my environment.

In that instant, I recognized with ferocious clarity how severely limited my world and my mind had been. Inspiration, that divine breath, rushed into my soul that evening, and when I left the computer I was not the same person as when I had sat down. I would get to America, land of opportunity and reinvention. I would apply to Harvard. I would become an educated person. I would learn to read books. I would teach myself how to speak, how to write, how to think. I would make myself useful. I would study my way out.

It was insane and irrational, but I decided to apply to Harvard. This was the only way I could prove to myself—and to the world— that I was worthy. I would rewrite my own story from scratch. As I walked slowly to my room, hearing the crickets chirping outside, the earth beneath my feet shook.

My former identity flashed and faded, and a new dream took its place. I had begun the journey of self-education that would change me for good.

. . .

When I awoke the next morning, I rushed out of bed to get to school. I was worried that this obsession with learning would be short-lived, that reality would deal my new dreams a fatal blow. I thought of giving up before I started. I nearly did.

There were standardized exams to study for, classes to attend, homework to complete. I still had average grades. I had never read a book from cover to cover. Yet I was energized by the challenge. Harvard? Why not me? If Obama could rise above his condition, why couldn't I?

In school, I sat at the front of the class and took careful notes. My teachers were initially amused by my seriousness, but I was fanatically committed to learning now. I was craving knowledge like a boy who had been in the desert for years, his throat parched with heat, only to find that a stream of water had been under him the entire time. *Build your vocabulary. You have potential.* These were no longer empty words to me.

After class, I rushed to the library to begin studying for the SATs. I looked up other colleges in places with strange names, New Haven and Princeton and Dartmouth, feeling ignorant at my limited mental geography that did not go farther than Toronto and Binghamton. And when I realized how much work went into simply applying to an American college, I felt the enormity of the task ahead. There was so much to learn, so much I did not know, so many boxes to check that I wondered if other children prepared for college when they were still in diapers. When school was let out, I ran to my room to finish all my schoolwork and resume my studying.

There were so many words I did not understand. I could barely finish a reading-comprehension passage without exhausting myself. Every day and night, I memorized vocabulary lists. I neatly copied out each word into my notebook, looked up the definition, then recited it aloud. My writing was so poor that I could barely keep my pencil from shaking after a few minutes. And the words themselves were complex, like *facetious* and *egregious*, this new lexicon alien to me. It amazed me how many words there were to learn.

I was running on pure adrenaline now. Hour after hour, day after day, I began teaching myself a whole new universe of language. I was energized by the fact that my vocabulary was growing, that I was gradually learning how to express myself.

These standardized exams were also my first introduction to American history. I was shocked to read about the Revolution, how a ragtag group of colonies had taken down the mightiest empire in the world. For me, the American story was an underdog's tale of perseverance against the odds, which was also Obama's narrative of rising beyond what was expected of him. I had a boyish romance with the myths of the United States.

But I did not tell anyone at school about my university ambitions. They would mock me and say I was getting a big head, and why not chill with the boys instead? Dreams still in infancy had to be protected. When they asked me what I was doing, I simply replied, "Studying," and left it at that. My nerves were too raw and my feelings too sensitive that a cutting remark by one of my peers might make me doubt what little faith I had in getting to college.

At home, it was my mother who noticed the changes first.

"Before you never study, now all you do is study," she said.

When my father learned of my ambitions to apply to Harvard, he simply asked, "But isn't that too high for you?" His comment stung. Even if he was right, I didn't want to hear it from him. I felt that there was a great conspiracy to keep me in my place, locked in the neighborhood forever.

My brother Oz was the most surprised by my sudden turn. He had seen me suffer through awful grades and beatings, and now was perplexed at how this radical shift had happened. I think he began viewing me as an actual older brother.

"You okay?" he asked one day. "You've gotten, like, possessed."

"I'm good," I said, putting my head back down.

In seeking out a new kind of life, I was consciously rejecting my family, my neighborhood, my culture and community. I wanted to be everything they were not: well-read, cosmopolitan, English-speaking, secular. My shame was mutating into determination, even if I despaired alone in my thoughts at night. Sometimes, all I did was despair. And whenever I felt hopeless, it was Amma who hushed me. The former teacher. She came to my rescue whenever our busted-up printer broke the night before an assignment was due, driving me past midnight to the FedEx store, in freezing temperatures, to get the assignment printed. She knew I had no room for error. It was Amma who reminded me daily to have faith, that dreams were accomplished only with great struggle, over many hours and months.

"Do not worry, *beta*," Amma said. "Whatever is for your betterment, Allah will make that happen."

• • •

Over the next months, I ignored everyone at school, including Erica. I studied, I read books, and during breaks at school, rather than hang out with friends, I read the newspaper by myself on the bench. This was how I came to see in the *Toronto Star* that my old friend Shilton had been killed.

"Youth, 17, Killed in Police Chase." A picture of a car in flames and a short write-up underneath. Shilton had died in a police chase just days before his seventeenth birthday. We had not spoken since I left Scartown, but we had been close since we were children. Now he was dead.

I sat there, pale-faced, unable to think amid the passing voices around me. Scenes from a forgotten past floated through my mind like moments from a dream: riding our bikes as children; running through the grassy fields on summer afternoons; rapping and singing together and goofing around with inside jokes. I saw Shilton's purple bike, his beautiful smile, the way he had said to me, in the principal's office one day in fifth grade, "Don't you sometimes wish you could fast-forward time just to see what mistakes you've made, so you can come back and not make them?" If only we had known that some of us did not have the luxury of second chances.

The unfairness of life had always been around me, but I was acutely aware of it now, how a rapid decision could change everything. When young men died, it was always their redeeming qualities that were memorialized: he had gone to college, he had been a star athlete, had served in the armed forces. But Shilton was not even an adult and had been killed before he had the chance to pursue his dreams. Shilton was gone now—and would take with him all the hopes his own immigrant parents had carried. Another truth revealed itself: that the world, our world, was cruel and our lives could be taken without explanation.

The day Shilton was buried, I told myself I would never give up and would always protect my body.

Now my academic focus grew into a deeper obsession. I kept

studying and my numbers crept upward, my vocabulary deepened. My mission was driving me forward, even though I had a nagging suspicion that no amount of time would compensate for all the years I had wasted.

"Keep the faith," I whispered. Preparation, practice, and patience were what I needed. The first two I had willed myself to possess, but patience I did not have. What I had in abundance was the immigrant boy's willingness to eat pain and keep going.

I needed an education.

I needed a new life.

I needed, wanted, needed to be somebody else. I needed to be wanted by the world. And if I couldn't be somebody the world wanted, I would make myself into somebody the world needed. I felt the pull of my community backward and the pull of the outside world forward, equally forceful, demanding that I change. I needed to escape my neighborhood. I needed to become free.

10.

Dream of a Glorious Escape

That January, four months after my epiphany, I was informed by Harvard that I was to be interviewed in a downtown Toronto law office. The partner worked for the biggest firm in the country—yes, they interviewed everyone, but I saw this as a good sign. I was ecstatic as I thought of going into the big city, only to realize all too late that I had communicated with the big city lawyer with my "Yung O" email address.

Dada helped me with my tie. I put on the secondhand suit he gave me, a woolly and ill-fitting outfit with the shoulders bunched up and the cuffs too tight. My father claimed the suit was made in Italy, but the inside flap clearly said Shaukat&Shaukat, Islamabad, Pakistan.

Looking at myself in the mirror, at my round eyes, at my clear brown skin, at the light stubble forming on my cheeks, I mouthed the phrases I had been practicing.

Yes, sir, I am honored to be here. Yes, sir, I know how to study. No, I have never committed a crime. Yes, I am able to learn quickly.

I put aftershave on my face, since an online magazine said this was what a young man should do before an interview. I did not want the big lawyer smelling curry on my clothes.

In the mirror, I recited some vocabulary words I had learned: *cultivate, luminous, stellar.* Staring at myself, I repeated the last word like an incantation: *s-t-e-l-l-a-r.* Was I pronouncing it correctly? Or was it one of the many words I had read but not heard, and the minute I spoke it I would be revealed as a fraud?

What is your name?

Omer, sir.

I pronounced it as whitely as I could. *Oh-mer. O-mer. Like Homer without the* H.

It was a cold Saturday morning with a gray sky when me and Dada got on the highway. I sat in the passenger seat with my folder and a pen. The folder held a résumé and copies of my report card, with grades that were now in the A range and comments from teachers that said my improvement was the best they had seen in years. I stared out the window, gripping my folder tightly. The 401 was a jammed-up highway and I counted down the minutes before I would officially be late. The car nearly broke down on the way and we had to pull to the side of the road so Dada could check the engine.

"Bloody mechanic says he fixed the problem and still it is there." He began muttering about how he would go and give the mechanic a piece of his mind and I grew tense. I saw it as a bad omen.

We got back on the road, sputtering toward the city. We arrived downtown just in time, and I marveled at the gleaming skyscrapers. I had only ever seen these tall buildings from afar.

"This is the Financial District," Dada said. "Lots of money here."

He parked by the side of a giant black tower that looked imposing and scary, like it was out of *The Lord of the Rings.*

"I will do a circle like this," he said, motioning with his hands, "and then I will wait here for you. Good luck, *beta.*"

My nerves twitched. As I walked up the stone steps, I wondered if my father had been right, whether I was aiming too high. I would be the first in my family to go to college in the West, and now I wondered whether all this wasn't a little crazy. *You've been a fuckup your whole life. This won't change nothing.* My inner demon was speaking. Maybe I should be more "realistic," I thought. No. Being realistic was not in my nature anymore.

Entering through the glass doors, I approached the person at the front desk. I gave her my name. Powerful-looking people in suits whisked by into elevators. The sounds of briefcases swinging, phones ringing, heels clacking echoed in the foyer. The glass panels were all so magnificent. How did these people work here?

"Mr. Hall will be right with you," said the receptionist. "You can have a seat."

I glided over to the smooth leather sofa, sat down, and adjusted my legs three times, pretending that I belonged. I fixed my tie. I glanced at my transcript. I tried not to appear too amazed at the sight of these smart-looking white faces moving past me. They were all so beautiful: the women walked confidently like they were in command. Did these people all go to university? Did they study to become lawyers and get good jobs here and get to work in the skyscraper? I was only fifteen miles from home, but geographically and psychologically, I was sitting in a totally different world, lacking the correct papers and proper qualifications.

My hands got sweaty and I grew faint at the idea that I was in over my head.

In a moment that would repeat itself many times over, I recognized the enormous gulf between this world of suits and knowledge and professional degrees—the world of power, which was white and handsome—that separated this segregated palace of riches from my own community. I felt like a boy who had snuck out of his village in the middle of the day and wandered into the wrong room, wearing the wrong clothes and the wrong skin.

I thought of my mother. She had been a teacher, hadn't she? But that was in Pakistan, in a remote town, no less. She preferred to speak Urdu; when she spoke English, her words were thickly accented. I mouthed some vocabulary words and made sure my English was correct.

My eyes wandered to the glass door. My thoughts became blurry. *Should I just get up and leave now, tell my father there's been a misunderstanding and Mr. Hall was busy?*

I looked down at my hands, at my starchy suit, at my unpolished shoes. What was I doing here? A self-critical voice echoed in my ears, the inner impostor.

The voice repeated these warnings and concluded with a threat: *Today is the day you will be found out.*

I eyed the door. It was only a few feet away.

I became so lost in my internal monologue that I didn't hear the voice calling to me.

"Ahem, Omer?"

A tall gray-haired man with prominent eyes extended his hand. "Geoff. Pleased to meet you. Shall we?"

He led me to an elevator. Geoff made a comment about the building and I smiled awkwardly.

"Are you interested in architecture?" he asked.

"Yes, sir," I said, although I knew nothing about the subject.

"Please just call me Geoff."

We rode up in silence after that. I followed Geoff through the winding law firm corridors, through a golden library filled with stacks of law books. I tried to act like all this was familiar to me, concealing my awe at the splendor around me.

"Do you spend a lot of time here?" I asked.

Geoff laughed as we walked. "Not as much as I used to."

He led me into a small room with a window. The fog was thick over Toronto, but I was standing high above the entire city. If I squinted hard enough, I could see my old world of Scartown in the distance.

"So," Geoff said, "why don't you tell me a bit about yourself."

"Sure," I said and started rattling off incoherent details about my life. Later, I would learn that there was a technique to answering such questions, that the best answers were not the result of improvisation but calculated practice. I would learn that when someone said, *Tell me your story*, they were expecting a succinct answer that grabbed their attention, had a clear beginning, middle, and end, and was told in under one minute—and they didn't literally mean for you to tell them everything. But I was young and uneducated to the fact that in this gilded world there were special codes of thought and communication.

I started at the beginning and went on for some minutes.

"I see," Geoff said, taking notes. "Do you see yourself as a leader?"

"Yes," I answered. "I think I can lead."

Geoff's eyebrows went up. "You *think*?"

"I mean, I know."

He noted it down. We spent some time talking about politics and what I wanted to do.

"I want to be a lawyer," I said. It was blurted out like an accidental confession. I told Geoff that Obama had inspired me to start reading and getting serious about books.

"As it happens," Geoff said, "I met him at Harvard."

"Really?" I said.

"Yes. He graduated a couple years ahead of me. You should read his book, *Dreams from My Father.*"

"I have it in my bag right here," I said.

"Good, very good."

His words were an intoxicant. If only I could tell Geoff how badly I wanted to prove myself, to show the world that I wasn't a failure. Every gesture, every word, every intonation, every shift in my hands, every movement I tried to plan one step in advance so he believed he was speaking to a student with potential.

"Well," Geoff said. "Thank you for coming. I hope to write a fair and favorable review."

He smiled, said goodbye. I walked out of the building and knew it had not gone well.

Dada was in his car right where he said he would be, chewing on paan and talking loudly in Urdu on his cell phone.

I got in the car, slumped down silently, stared out at the giant black tower. We drove to the sound of Punjabi radio.

A few weeks later, the rejection from Harvard arrived by mail.

...

The letter devastated me. I shut myself in my room for days, wondering whether to apply to other colleges. The rejection was like all the report cards I had gotten before this year, when the teacher gave me the envelope facedown. I was heartbroken, though I should have seen it coming.

Because I was innocent, I did not appreciate the huge gap between where I was starting and where I was aiming. Despite the disappointment, I learned a valuable lesson: there was a cost to being unprepared.

I accepted my fate. I promised myself I would work harder.

A month later, I told my guidance counselor what had happened. He smiled knowingly. A pudgy man with a red goatee, he leaned forward as if revealing the pathway to a hidden door.

"I'll let you in on a secret," he said. "There's a proper university three hours east where all the rich kids from Canada go before they head off to America and England. It's called Queen's. Go there. You'll learn a lot."

Instead of wallowing in my grief, I put in my application and kept studying. At home, gravity pulled me backward. As soon as the relatives heard that I would go away for university, they began their whispering campaign. Iqbal Mian was regularly twisting his mustache and uttering warnings. Don't send him away, said one auntee. He will become a *gora*, a drinker, sleeping with white girls.

For this reason, my parents tried to keep my plans away from the family. I later realized they were not merely thwarting the collective shame of another rejection, but also protecting me. If there was one thing Brown people were good at, my father once said, it was bringing each other down.

Iqbal Mian was at our house one day in March when I took a break from my eight-hour marathon studying for exams.

He glared at me, set his cup of chai down.

"Have you gotten a scholarship?" he asked in front of my parents.

"I'm still trying," I said, wanting to be vague.

"*Chalo,*" he said nonchalantly. "Without a scholarship, there is not even a point of going." Then he listed off all the wonderful things *his* kids were doing.

I cringed at the arrogance.

"You want to be *Angrez*?" Iqbal Mian asked, referring to white people. "You want to get a fancy education and leave us and commit sins?"

"That's not true," I said.

"Do not leave," he said. "Stay here."

My old anger was stirring. But I stayed quiet. In Urdu, there was a fine balance between haughtiness and politeness. It was so subtle that it could not be challenged, especially from a boy of not-eighteen to an older uncle.

My brother Oz nudged me. He whispered, "An uncle with no education is telling you where to get yours."

We both laughed.

Brown Boy

"What's so funny?" Iqbal Mian shouted.

"Nothing," we both said. Nothing at all.

• • •

In the last days of that semester, I got the acceptance letter from Queen's. There was a scholarship attached. I had to reread the letter four times just to make sure there wasn't a catch. Here was the golden ticket I had desperately wanted. Far from diminishing my dreams, the rejection from Harvard had set me on the path I would take. It energized me. Amma insisted on donating to the mosque for good fortune. Dadiye blessed my forehead with a prayer. Dada simply wanted to know how much the scholarship was worth.

I felt that I had accomplished something for the first time in my life, but I did not allow myself any celebration. I had failed throughout my entire upbringing—failed at school, at being tough, and did not fully trust myself. I was far behind my peers, and college would be a challenge. Still, as I stepped out my front door and walked around the block, I had that eerie sensation that life would be starting over again in the fall. I would leave my neighborhood with a blank slate, a blank face, construct myself anew.

I walked toward the old fields and the basketball court where I had witnessed so many brawls, wasting hours away. Rather than a moment of calm to reflect on my acceptance, I felt a tremor of panic. A commotion was starting on the soccer field.

Another big fight was about to happen. I clutched the scholarship letter, watching as boys poured in from the sidewalks and streets, some with baseball bats in their hands. I didn't want to be there. But I found myself in a position that would become familiar: standing at the edges and serving as a witness to the chaos around me.

Two groups of boys approached one another like warring armies. There must have been a hundred bodies on the soccer field now. Insults were shrieked. One boy jumped atop another. Mayhem ensued, all the boys began attacking and punching and kicking each other. One boy struck another with a baseball bat, and the wounded boy crumpled as if falling into prayer.

I saw Indian and Pakistani shop owners from across the street come outside to see what was going on. The uncles and auntees shook their heads in our direction, disappointment seared across their faces. We were their children. They were our fathers and mothers. And they all seemed to be saying, *Have you no shame? Is this why we came to this country?*

Here we were: the bastard sons of the West, congregating to destroy each other for sport in the middle of the afternoon. This was what the world wanted of us, to keep us fighting over petty beefs while the real power and knowledge and opportunities accumulated elsewhere, downtown, in the universities, in those jobs we would never get.

I saw the vice principals running toward the park. Sirens screeched in the distance. Two police cruisers swerved onto the grass, doors flying open, officers chasing after boys.

Fear moved me to action and I bolted as fast as I could, cutting through side streets, jumping over a fence, hopping across a backyard, my heart pounding, my legs moving on their own. The choices of my life flickered in my eyelids: the books or these streets, the future or the past, education or illiteracy, an elusive dream or being stuck here forever. I could feel the ghosts trailing behind me. And it was the electricity of these thoughts that made me run with decision. I was running toward a new life, running from this old world, running outside myself, running within myself. Running.

III.

White Masks

11.

Stranger in the Village

From what I could tell, very few Brown people had entered the town of Kingston, Ontario, across the river from New York State, when I showed up that fall. It was a place of history and monuments, with a university tucked into a corner by the lake. My first observations were that everyone was white: the security guards were white, the store owners were white, the police officers were white, the professors were white, the townsfolk were white, and of course, the students were white. I was stepping into a totally alien world.

The campus had old limestone buildings that gave the feeling of Oxbridge; clear fields and wide roads; a modern library. As soon as I stepped foot into this historic little community—inspired by the Scottish and English—I got the impression that outsiders were unwanted.

"Salma!" Dada said, carrying one of my bags up to my dorm. "You have put ten kilos in the suitcase for what?"

"He needs food," she answered. Amma had packed frozen tandoori chicken, rice, kebabs, daal, naan, roti, chutney into packets I could easily heat up. Some bags were marked FRIDGE while others said FREEZER. Even with a cafeteria within walking distance, Amma worried I would not be able to eat the food available to me.

Upstairs, down a hallway painted beige, we arrived to my new room. It had two desks and a bunk bed, a tiny television hanging from the corner. The room was covered in dust, with a low ceiling that was gray, giving the feel of a boarding school. I noticed some of my roommate's belongings, books by authors I had never heard of before: Bertrand Russell, James Joyce, John Stuart Mill, and several leather-bound books that said *Harvard Classics* on the spine.

Amma eyed the bottle of Irish whiskey on the table like it was a loaded shotgun.

"Beta," she said, "do not drink this alcohol."

I promised I wouldn't. Amma insisted that I have excess cleaning supplies and excessive snacks to keep me nourished. I would be alone for the first time in my life. She also brought out a little plastic jug from the suitcase. This was the all-important *lota*, or washing vessel, used to fulfill Islamic cleansing rituals.

My father smiled when he saw the jug.

"Yes, make sure to use your *lota*," Dada said, laughing. "These *goras* don't wash their asses after shitting!"

Amma was not impressed. "Be respectful," she chided.

We set up my room and then went to the cafeteria to eat. Dada had a burger. Amma did not touch the meat, opting only for a stale salad. Eating in silence, I observed the faces around me. They were white and at ease. It hit me that I would be stuck here, in a place where no one looked like me, in a town where I felt foreign, for four whole years. I had come from a multicultural neighborhood and now would be left to the villagers of a whites-only universe, where segregation existed in practice, if not in theory.

Evening fell, and soon I was walking my parents downstairs and out to the parking lot. I felt contradictory emotions: I wanted them to leave so I could begin my new life, but I did not want to be abandoned here to all the white people who made me afraid. I walked outside slowly. My parents could not sense the turmoil beneath my face.

We stood at the steps. Amma gave me a tearful hug. "Remember one thing," she said. "Education is not only about studying, it's about learning character."

Dada shook my hand. "Okay, okay, okay," he said with a one-armed hug. "You are here to study, not party. Keep your focus on the studies."

They got into the car, arguing over some trivial matter, and began to drive away. The engine sputtered into the quiet night. I stood there and watched my parents disappear, wishing that I had told them for once in my life that I loved them and missed them already.

. . .

Alcohol was in the air we breathed at Queen's. Other colleges might have prided themselves on their beer-guzzling festivities, but here the entire culture revolved around drinking. Orientation week consisted of swigging enough liquor to tranquilize a small horse, and then participating in one of the bizarre rituals of chanting in a language I did not know, a language called Gaelic, in this city where bright colors were donned and howls were hooted throughout the day. To abstain from alcohol, as I tried to do, was to be an outcast and viewed with suspicion. I felt guilty when I wasn't working, and the Muslim in me did not trust the dark taverns where men gathered to drink.

I skipped most events and went right to the library. At the entrance, a young brown-skinned student with a clipboard spotted me and examined my face like he knew me.

"Are you Ismaili?" he asked.

I shook my head.

"Are you Shi'a?" he asked.

I paused. Something in the question alarmed me. Never before had I been asked which sectarian group of Muslims I belonged to, and the one time I heard my father answer this question, he simply said, "I am human."

"Are you Shi'a?" the man repeated.

"No," I said with sarcasm, "but I *do* have two brothers named Ali."

He looked confused. I walked into the library, where I spent the afternoon studying by myself, trying to prepare for the academic challenge while the drunken hollering echoed from the windows. At the end of a long workday, I walked back to the dorm, watching drunk white girls and boys struggling to stay on their feet. I would grab my basketball shoes and head to the gym and play for hours, feeling a sense of accomplishment by denying myself the pleasures of alcohol and fun.

In those early days, the isolation got to me. I had spent the majority of my life with people who either looked like me or had parallel experiences, and now I was all by myself. My first weeks passed in a mental fog, broken only by the blueness of the morning. Sometimes, I looked forward to the night because I would be unconscious for eight hours, able to escape into a dreamworld where I was not so different. I had wanted to leave home, and now I was homesick, craving the soft embrace of my grandmother, the random mutterings of my father, the warm Pakistani meals prepared by my mother. I missed all that had made me, and could not assimilate quickly into a new culture where I was expected to leave my roots behind. I was experiencing the beginnings of a depression that would periodically overwhelm my spirit, especially when my solitude grew too severe.

Something had to give. Just as migration came with beauty and pain, so, too, did education. I was removed from all that I had known, sticking out in every room, in every class, lost in this village where I did not belong.

. . .

One day, I found a card in my mailbox, an invitation to an exclusive reception for scholarship winners. I wore my father's secondhand suit, applied extra deodorant, and walked to the hall. The reception was in a large room in the middle of campus. Entering the banquet, I saw a chandelier, and under its light, young men in dark suits and women in dresses, silver-haired professors chatting with disciples, the spirit of merriment and wonder filling the room.

Piano music drifted through the party. There was the familiar feeling of being allowed into a secret dance. I took a deep breath. I whispered to myself that I belonged here, that I had the right to be here. I gulped down a glass of wine and my head felt lighter. I was levitating now, observing the people in the room. I watched how their hands moved when they spoke, how their faces nodded when they listened, how they made eye contact, and I was memorizing all these tiny gestures. Their sentences were complete, their paragraphs proper, and they spoke with an authority I could not fathom, as though being at the top was a birthright, an inheritance.

They asked questions of my background: Which letters did I bear? Which stamps of approval? Which private school had I attended? Oh, but I was from a public school, and therefore all my gestures were the result of deliberate practice, a million mental calculations happening all at once.

But it was their manners that held my gaze. They were carrying themselves with a mastery that suggested they were privy to certain truths unknown to the outside world.

How will I swim with these people? They speak better English than I can write.

We were forged by different circumstances and histories. The most privileged of them could falter and still land a job at their fathers' companies. If I got too complacent, I'd lose my scholarship and be right back in the old neighborhood.

After a few more drinks, I became energized by the thought of competing with the monied sons and daughters from private schools. Drunken glee consumed my thoughts. I decided I would *Yessir* and *Yes, ma'am* them all. I wanted to be one of them, yes: a young Brown man with a white mask. But first I had to alter my disguise so it became indistinguishable from my face.

Drink in hand, I was full of revolutionary fervor, ready to wage my own war of independence and become a republic of one: self-defining, self-sustaining, self-governing, self-creating. I would forget the past entirely and move upward in this big, white world.

...

A few days later, back in my dorm room, I spotted my roommate reading a book on the lower bunk. Darragh had a long face, dark brown hair, curious eyes. He was an Irish American from the suburbs of Boston, laid-back and exuberant.

"Hello, good sir," he said to me, raising his glass.

"What are you drinking?" I asked.

Darragh had brewed his own alcohol in our room, a kind of hard cider. He offered me a sip. I looked at it and waved the drink away. The homemade concoction had the pungent smell of urine.

My roommate was a curious sort of white guy, different from the others on campus. Maybe it was because he was Irish, or because he was American, that he was easier to talk to—his father, I learned, had been a musician in Belfast and was close to the founder of the Irish Republican Army. Darragh said, "Cheers" to me when I went to class, and was always provoking me in debates about religion and philosophy.

That afternoon, Darragh was slouched over, reading a book by someone named Oscar Wilde.

"Listen to this," he said. "'Religion does not help me. The faith that others give to what is unseen, I give to what one can touch and look at. . . . When I think about religion at all, I feel as if I would like to found an order for those who *cannot* believe: the Confraternity of the Faithless, one might call it.'"

I sat back in my chair, trying to decipher these words. Finally, I asked him to explain what they meant.

"Oscar Wilde's an atheist," Darragh said. "He's condemning the stupidity of Christian dogma."

I nodded, unsure how to respond. A white person ripping on Christianity—was I supposed to agree with this, or merely listen? Was he testing me?

"Frankly," Darragh continued, "I think all religion is ridiculous and violent and there's no such thing as God."

I sat up in my seat. I felt the provocation in his voice. For the next few hours, we debated the existence of God. I wasn't religious, but now that my new friend was slandering monotheism—and soon, Islam in particular—I tried to defend the idea that God existed.

"How can you be so sure?" I asked. "Neither of us have come back from the dead to prove that there's no afterlife."

Darragh scoffed. "I haven't seen a pasta monster in the sky, either."

My nerves twitched. I took another approach.

"Look, wouldn't you rather believe there is a God, so if you're right, you end up in heaven, rather than believing there is nothing, and if you're wrong, you end up in hell?"

"Pascal's wager," Darragh said, giving name to the argument I had just tried. He was well-read, spoke clearly, like he had been having philosophical discussions for years. Me, I stammered my way through the conversation, having been silent for an equal number of years as elders shouted at each other over the dinner table about Pakistan and the CIA.

Our debates about the origin of the universe, about the end of times, about the existence of a Creator, soon became the talk of our floor. Other students joined in and we had these all-out, cage-match discussions that went on for hours. We'd even throw on a YouTube video—in the early days when YouTube was an enticing place of inquiry—and watch Christopher Hitchens, the witty author and intellectual, debate religion and God. Behind our closed door, we argued the night away, and our room became known as the place you went to have your arguments tested.

I had never openly questioned Allah or God in this way before— it was one of those points completely off the table in our Muslim home. Even if I agreed with the lack of concrete evidence for God, I felt the sting of personal rebuke in these debates, as three or four people attacked Islam as more pernicious than other religions. That the criticism of Islam was coming from a white person's mouth made me sit up, pay attention, feel my own ignorance against his learning—and I would go to the library for hours and study the great religious thinkers like Augustine and Aquinas, and the skeptics like Spinoza and Einstein, trying to understand rationally whether God could be defended. I studied Plato and his Allegory of the Cave, wondering whether I was moving toward the light or simply gawking at shadows. I studied Galileo and Copernicus and John Stuart Mill, and I began to comprehend that all these thinkers were having a centuries-long duel with each other over the fundamental questions of existence. Nothing was resolved. Nothing was certain. There were always counterarguments and rebuttals, more to read and study, each layer of knowledge opening new questions and subjects. Far from finding certainty, I began to fall in love with the questions themselves.

And I tried my best to check my identity at the door, not to take the critiques of my roommate or friends too personally. Yes, I was the only Muslim on our floor, one of the few non-white students on campus, but I told myself that a liberal education demanded a thick skin. Each time one of their points slashed through me, I bit my tongue and kept the conversation at the intellectual level, worrying that by taking it personally I was violating the sacred norms of debate. The point was to learn, to challenge others and be challenged in return.

Yet what was happening on campus around me made this separation of personal and political deeply difficult.

When I joined up with a local group of student debaters, they interrogated me about what I believed.

One boy named Sam pointed me out during a discussion about the Middle East: "So, you support Hamas?" he asked.

I was frozen. Another boy uttered the word "Islamofascism."

My feelings roiled beneath my skin. "No," I said defensively, "I *do not* support Hamas."

"But you're Muslim?" asked another student with blond hair. He jabbed his finger in my face. A dozen blue eyes blinked in my direction, the silence piercing my ears.

And then I said something that I would later regret. "I—I—I'm not Muslim," I said. "My parents are Muslim." All the way home, I felt an aching guilt in my throat, as though I had thrown my community under the bus just to seem more appealing to white people. I would soon learn that there was a whole range of subjects like al-Qaeda and Islam and religion and race and the War on Terror where I would have to keep myself under strict surveillance.

These conversations were not occurring in a vacuum. Political theory was not reality. The college darkened that fall with a series of racist incidents that targeted people of color and Muslims in particular. Someone had defaced the Muslim Student Association, broken into the Muslim worship area, and stolen the donation box. A campus leader who wore the hijab told the student paper that a group of men had driven past her the night before and one of them had shouted, "Let me unwrap you." While the college was reeling from these hateful incidents, someone had spray-painted the words *Should Die* over the word *Muslims* on a poster. I soon learned that many other Black, Brown, and Asian students here had been harassed or targeted either by the townsfolk or other students.

I was angry and didn't know what to do. I wanted to speak but could not find my words. I had come to believe that my feelings did not matter in this world, that my opinions were secondary to theirs. I had been taught that I did not have the right to feel hurt.

I thought of Malcolm X, wondering what he would say if he could speak to us. Would Malcolm tell us we were being insulted because we did not respect ourselves? Would he tell us that we had unconsciously accepted the double standards of collective guilt for us, but individual differentiation for them? Would Malcolm remind us that white supremacy had taught us to hate ourselves and accept second-class status while sheltering others from criticism, protecting them with money and institutional power? I thought back to the boy I had been on 9/11, confused, fearful, and anxious. Now I was thrust into a world where I was seen as the interloper, the enemy, and I had to watch my back.

But I stayed silent, moved quietly, stuck to my books. The answer to racism, I believed, was to outwork the racists. I never stopped being on high alert. Late at night, walking back from a lecture, I checked twice over my shoulder when I found myself on a dark street. I crept slowly, stealthily, moving between the library and the dorm under the cover of night. Then I went to bed and tossed and turned for hours, having arguments with white phantoms.

When morning arrived, motivation was beating in my chest. I rushed down Princess Street in a hurry, returning to my temple, to my safe space: the library.

12.

Golden Era

In my second year of college, I redrew the map of the future. I saw what Queen's had to offer and wanted more. The books I read introduced me to the great Western thinkers, and I wondered what Paris was like, whether I might study there, and what about London, and then America? Sometimes, thinking about all these places filled me with such excitement that I forgot where I was standing. Then a long, inevitable frustration set in as I realized the gap between where I was and where I wanted to be. I felt limited and provincial. I had no personal exposure to Europe and felt the urgent need to get there, the land where the Renaissance and the Enlightenment had taken place, where the ideas of liberalism and democracy were born. As the history books reminded me, Europe was the center of civilization itself.

I had done well in my first year, had read a lot, studied hard, and spent every free second with my nose in a book. Beneath the determination, though, my spirit was unsettled. That summer, after Erica had broken up with me, I spent most of my time alone. Away from family, living in Ottawa as a political intern, I was hurt and isolated. When my mother called, she scolded me about not praying enough. Amma was worried that the philosophy I was studying in college was turning me into an atheist. It was the furthest thing from my mind as I sat in a humid apartment. I wish I could have talked to Amma or Dada, but it was impossible. Friends from the old neighborhood called to tell me that Gurpreet had been killed by a drunk driver, that Brandon had been stabbed to death, that Lukas had been taken by a speeding sheet of metal. Kids at eighteen, nineteen, were attending more funerals than celebrations. All these losses weighed on me.

And to Amma's credit, she was correct in her motherly guess that I was doubting whether God or Allah even existed. Where was God in my life? He had been rationally questioned into the background.

Yet one day that summer, out of sheer despair, I decided to walk to the local church in Ottawa. The church was made of stone with a steeple pointing to the heavens. I went inside after some trepidation—never had I been inside a church before. I knew that in Islam the Gospels and message of Jesus were respected, and that Jesus was also considered a prophet. He was respected with the same deference given to the Torah and the messenger Abraham.

I saw a giant BOOK SALE sign at the entrance to the church and immediately went downstairs to the basement. Rows and rows of books. I bought Dickens and Gandhi and made sure to take a King James Bible back home with me.

Every night that summer, when my loneliness made me want to lie down and not get up from bed, I would read bits of the Bible. In this way, I read the entirety of the Old Testament and the Gospels, slowly, carefully, always after a pang of distress disturbed my thoughts. I saw myself as a Westerner and knew that Christianity was the religion of the West, its heritage and inheritance, made known in every monument, university, parliament, and town. I felt invested in the Bible and found in it stories that were familiar to me.

But it was the person of Jesus Christ that absorbed me the most. I had learned that Jesus was actually named Yeshua, that he was a Jewish preacher from Palestine and a dissident put to death for treason. Even his skin color would have been closer to olive or brown, and his language Aramaic. When I returned to the church that Sunday for my first-ever service, I looked up at the slim white body on the cross, and wondered what he would make of the world made in his name. I did not yet know the real history of the West, only that the West was glorious, and founded upon the rock laid by the messenger on the cross.

That summer, Christianity and Christ kept my mind working through dark tunnels. I did not convert to Christianity, and the church only temporarily lifted the feelings of isolation, but there was comfort in the community I found. I was still searching, still looking, and felt that I had more to see and do. Soon I was back at college in the fall, itching again to escape, wanting to run to Europe—and still shadowed by deeper questions I could not yet answer.

• • •

One afternoon at the start of sophomore year, I was in the library studying Kant and listening to Kanye when I looked up and saw a woman looking back at me. She had brown eyes and brown skin and dark brown hair. She looked like she could have been from anywhere, the Philippines or the Punjab.

"Are you in politics?" she asked.

I nervously assumed she was talking to someone else.

"No, you," she said.

"Me?"

"The ghost behind you."

I blushed. "Yes . . . politics."

She asked me my name. I spoke so quickly, my name came out garbled.

"Do you always look so lost?" she said, smiling.

"Yes, I mean, no."

We made small talk. Her name was Sheela, a beautiful woman from Toronto. As it turned out, we were the same year, the same major, in the same classes. It was a big city that we came from, but it also felt like the smallest place on earth. Sheela was the opposite of the girls I had known: well-traveled, worldly, with a certain upper-class elegance.

She said, "I want to go to law school in America," and my eyes lit up with recognition. We walked over to a burger joint on campus, Sheela strutting comfortably, leather bag on her shoulder. She looked like some kind of corporate executive in the making, a woman who seemed to flow through this world as if it belonged to her.

Over burgers, we talked about our lives.

"Do white people think *you're* exotic, too?" she asked.

"I don't think so," I said. "They just see me as different."

"Do you think you'll end up in law school?"

"I hope so," I said. "What about you?"

"I want to go, but you know Brown parents and their daughters."

She raised an eyebrow, and I immediately knew what she was talking about.

Sheela said, "They want me to get married. My parents need grandchildren, you know." I waited a moment, then she threw out the words "Just joking," but I could sense a nervousness beneath her laughter.

Over the next weeks, we texted and texted, the wait between messages agonizing. Even after I kissed her, we did not define our relationship. We were two lost students in a college where newfangled terms for love were cooked up daily: FWBs, FBs; the undefined nature of relationships cushioning young men and women from having to deal with commitment.

Later that week, Sheela invited me to join her at a sushi restaurant off campus. My nerves were a wreck, never having eaten sushi— *kachi machli*, as my mother said, uncooked fish.

When I walked in the dimly lit restaurant, Sheela sat at a table, texting with a smile.

"You're late," she said.

"Sorry."

I sat down and scanned the menu. Everything was too expensive for me. The words were all in Japanese and I was confused by the pictures. Already, the week before, my debit card had been declined at the ATM. I was perpetually low on cash and either ate noodles in my room, canned tuna, or one of the bags of frozen food my mother had given me.

Sheela flipped over my menu to the English side.

"There," she said.

I ordered the cheapest dish I saw, and when it was brought over—a sliver of pink fish over some white rice—I tried to use chopsticks before dropping them in frustration for a fork.

"So," she said, "my parents want me to fly to Dubai this weekend to help with the family business."

"Dubai . . ." I said, nodding, forgetting to act normal.

"Yeah, our family has this company so I travel a lot. You know, London, Madrid, the Emirates. Have you ever been to Europe?"

I shook my head.

"Well, you *must* go. It's such a fabulous place."

With what money? I thought. It wasn't as if I could snap my fingers and end up across the Atlantic Ocean. I would have to apply for an exchange program, apply for student loans, apply for scholarships, and even then it might not be enough. I didn't have the heart to tell Sheela I had never even been on an airplane as an adult.

"My family," she said with a sigh. "They have lots of expectations of me. When you're a Brown girl, you can't just live for yourself."

She told me about her father's export company, how they flew in first class. But when Sheela mentioned her family's history, I knew there was more than what I saw on her confident face. Her parents were of different faiths, Hindu and Sikh, a West Indian and a Punjabi. Her grandparents had rejected the union, but her parents had gone ahead anyway. Now, feeling family pressure, Sheela said she wanted to get married to a man from her "culture"—a word she would return to—sooner rather than later.

We're twenty, I thought.

Sheela picked at her sushi. Her ideas swung wildly from her parents' background to the things she could buy with money, as if money were the salvation, the way books were for me.

"I like the finer things in life," she said. "Like LV."

"LV?" I asked. "What's that?"

"Louis Vuitton. I enjoy couture and fashion."

Sheela was speaking in tongues: *sushi*, *LV*, *couture* were words I had never heard before.

"Did you buy your own LV?" I asked innocently.

After a brief pause, she yelled out: "*Yes!*"

Her attachment to money didn't strike me as vain; if anything, coming from my background, it made her even more attractive. Money was how she signaled status, and status mattered in Brown families just like in white ones. But I didn't yet understand that constantly talking about brands was itself a sign of insecurity.

When the waiter brought over two checks, I wanted to hug him. After paying for my meal, I had less than ten dollars in my account.

"What do your parents do, by the way?" she asked, looking up at me from her phone.

She had touched on a sore spot. I didn't want her thinking less of me because my parents did not have the professional jobs and wealth of her own family.

"They work for the government," I said.

I felt the sting of this lie in my throat.

"Interesting," she said.

· · ·

Over the next months, we spent every minute together, working on papers, talking about the white people around us, Sheela regaling me with stories of her travels: the prince who had hit on her in London, the hobnobbing with CEOs and other influential people. For reasons I could not discern, she seemed most interested in seeing me when there was an assignment due, and I was just happy to be in her presence. Sheela was one of those pretty girls who knew she was pretty. She moved through the world with an ease I did not possess. My brown skin was an armor and a shield, one that I hid behind and concealed from myself. Hers was like a shining light. When she used the word *culture*, she did so with personal pride.

Every time Sheela asked about my origins, I lied to her or changed the subject.

We were sitting by the fireplace that December in her dorm building when she broached the subject again.

"Are your parents super Muslim?" she asked.

"No," I shot back.

She fidgeted with her pen. A Chinese student wandered in, sensed the tension, and left.

"My friend dated a Muslim once. Everything was fine until they got married, then he got all crazy."

I tried to shrug this off. "Not everyone's like that."

"In my culture, people tend to marry only in the same circles," she said.

There was that word again. Anytime Sheela said "culture," there was an air of exclusive possession. To her, "culture" meant being Hindu or Sikh, not Muslim, even though both mine and Sheela's forefathers had come from the same place. I did not appreciate that my own grandmother had lived in Amritsar and that Muslims, Hindus, and Sikhs had all once been brothers and sisters. But Sheela saw things differently. When she spoke of "culture," she meant a single box around her that defined her by religion and ethnicity: Sikh, Indian, Punjabi.

When I said "culture," I meant that we were both Brown, yes, but we were *born in the West*. That meant a certain freedom, an autonomy in how to live that none of our cousins back in South Asia would have had, that our parents never have had.

Sheela rotated her ring nervously. "I just . . . I can't be with a Muslim," she said. "My parents expect me to be with someone from my culture."

Her confession stung me.

"But we're the same culture!" I said.

She didn't need to say any more. I knew we were battling the ghosts of 1947, the great bloodbath known as Partition, a history that was still unknown to me. I began to understand that no relationship would ever succeed between us, because for Sheela's family, Muslims were an ancestral enemy. To tell the truth, my own family would have recoiled had I brought a Hindu-Sikh girl home. I knew that uncles often made offhanded comments about Hindus, as if the two peoples were from different planets rather than being neighbors, and that Hindus, when marrying, inquired often about the person's caste, just as Muslims assumed you would marry another believer.

But all those differences can be conquered. It wasn't just culture or religion that separated me from Sheela and her family as much as social class: I did not have the sophistication to move in her world, and this alone made me feel shame.

Still, we kept seeing each other. She was a Brown girl, and I thought I loved her, was infatuated by her, was in love with my ideas of her. But my fate was to sense the ending at the beginning. Like anyone new to these raw emotions, I was blind to what was right in front of my eyes. It was a great fault of mine, one I would struggle with as an adult: wanting the love of the very people who could never love me back.

I still had to grow up—and growing up was a very hard thing to do.

. . .

A few weeks later, I was in the library stacks late at night. The February cold gave the warmth of the library even more appeal. Between the insecurities I felt about culture and class around Sheela, and all my studies filled with European thinkers, I did not have the faintest clue about who I was or where I had come from. Sheela was more like the white students in this respect, who could tell me, with frightening precision, when Grandad or Great-Granddad had settled in North America, which town they called home, which army regiments they had served in during the world wars. It was as if everyone was able to trace their lineage and claim a piece of history, but I could see no further back than Scartown.

Who was I? What was my community?

My eyes scanned the books on the shelves, light glinting off the pages.

It was then that a book called out to me and I plucked it from the shelf, intrigued by the title.

Invisible Man.

I wiped the dust off the cover and opened to the first page.

"I am an invisible man," wrote the nameless narrator. "I am a man of substance, of flesh and bone, fiber and liquids—and I might even be said to possess a mind."

The author was not H. G. Wells, but Ralph Waldo Ellison, a Black man from Oklahoma. I was pulled in by the music of his words, the sharp feeling of recognition, and I sat down right there in the stacks and continued reading.

"All my life I had been looking for something, and everywhere I turned someone tried to tell me what it was. . . . I was naïve. I was looking for myself and asking everyone except myself questions which I, and only I, could answer."

When I looked up, a whole lifetime seemed to have passed. I left the library and went back to my apartment and read late into the night about this strange, quixotic, and hilarious man whom others misperceive.

The invisible man reached out of the book and grabbed me by my shirt, shook me, and asked in that voice laden with irony: *Who the hell are you?*

I began pacing in the room. I asked myself: *Where did you come from? Who were your people? What was your past?* I could not have been a blank slate, born without context. And when no answers were forthcoming, I panicked.

The invisible man's voice was in my ears: *But how the hell can you know where you're going if you don't know who you are?*

There was no one I could call. Not my parents, who I hadn't spoken to in months. We no longer understood each other, and I would not get any clear answers from them. Their answers, shaped by their own migrations, would be in contradiction and even self-contradictory.

I rang up the one person who might understand the crisis I was having without judging me. Sheruu Bhai was the person I trusted in my moment of vulnerability. Months had passed since we'd last spoken, but we had never lost touch, not even after some in the family had shunned him. Sheruu was now in Pakistan working as a commercial pilot.

The phone rang for a long time.

"Ah-lo?" he finally said.

"I need to know something," I said feverishly. I skipped with the niceties and got right to the point. "Who are we?"

"What do you mean?" he asked.

"I mean, who are we? I don't know anything. I don't know shit about myself. No one ever told me."

There was a long pause on the other end of the line. Sheruu did not ask where the question was coming from. Perhaps he heard the urgency in my voice and recognized it from his own past, as a child of two continents, raised without a father, forced to piece together two halves of a history that did not quite fit.

"Well," he said, "I don't know where to begin."

He patiently walked me through some of our history, how our father had been born in Pakistan, a nation created in 1947, how our grandfather had been from British India, a respected man in his town whose memory was still kept alive. He told me what little he knew about my mother's family and their village. The family's migration to the new world, and before this, the journey across the bloody borders of India. He named the different towns, our father's family in Wah Cantt, my mother's in Murree, and the city of Lahore, where my grandmother once called home. I was most intrigued by my mother's origins—her village—but my brother had to go.

We hung up. I held the phone as I sat in silence, but the drumbeat of the invisible man's questions still lingered. Sheruu's story ended precisely where mine started, and I felt the gaps in the narrative that I would have to fill in myself.

The sun was rising outside my window. In that moment, I felt the painful birth of consciousness about identity. Who was this "I" and why did this "I" feel so artificial, so imposter-like, as if the "I" had to always beg for acceptance? Ellison would lead me to Richard Wright and James Baldwin and Toni Morrison and Frederick Douglass, each one of these thinkers becoming like my own family. I was not Black, but Black American literature would be my saving grace. Nor was I white, even if white European thinkers had constituted the entirety of my formal schooling. I was something in between, something amorphous, amphibious, a man who had to constantly improvise his name and his face in order to blend in.

. . .

Every day that semester, I returned to the library hungry for more truths. I sought out diverse writers and historians and novelists who could explain to me the layers of the past. I would arrive in the library, find a study carrel on the third floor, put my things down, and then disappear into the stacks, returning with armfuls of books. I read history, and Thoreau, and *The Denial of Death*. Books became escapes into other worlds that would refract back at me.

Each morning and night, I would sit down and begin to read, copying out full paragraphs in my notebook, referring to the text, jotting down the key authorities and arguments. In this way, I saw the holes in my education. I might have loved my Enlightenment philosophers, but where were the Africans? The Indians? The Chinese? The Arabs? What was happening around the world when Europe was mired in its Dark Ages? What was the true nature of the Crusades? What was the true history of slavery and why was it not taught? Where were the Muslims and why had Islam been erased from the curriculum? I was an investigator, piecing together a puzzle whose contents had been smashed and dispersed, seeking out a forbidden knowledge that the professors did not teach.

Some nights, I fell asleep in the library and the security guard had to wake me up and tell me the building was closed. I would take my bag of books and walk in the cold to my apartment, where I continued my independent study.

Eventually, I made a discovery of the Islamic past. There existed a period between the ninth and the thirteenth centuries when Muslim philosophers, theologians, mathematicians, mystics, poets, and polymaths were authoring the greatest literature in the world. They were translating and preserving the ancient Greeks, making quantum leaps in astronomy and medicine, writing long commentaries attempting to reconcile revelation with faith. Long debates took place in the court of the caliph, where the writings of Jewish, Roman, Greek, and Persian thinkers were assimilated. It was not a stretch to say that it was because of Islam's rich golden age that knowledge was reborn in the West, ushering in the Renaissance.

Al-Ma'mun was the caliph of Baghdad who patronized a school of rationalism that argued that reason must be applied to holy texts. In Baghdad there existed the House of Wisdom, then the largest library in the world, where the works of Plato and Aristotle and Hippocrates were translated, where al-Khwarizmi worked to found algebra and would lend his name to the word *algorithm*, where monumental treatises on ophthalmology and surgery and infections were composed. And it was not just Baghdad but also Damascus and Córdoba, Spain, and Iran where the great thinkers were having debates about every domain of knowledge. Some, like Ibn Sina, would write hundreds of books across all disciplines. From Persia to India, art and images were created that historians would study centuries later. A feast of intellect and imagination reigned in the Islamic past.

I had too many questions. I wondered how an Islam of such openness could exist centuries ago, while Baghdad in modern times remained a war-torn city, and jihadists had taken the place of scholars, claiming the mantle of the faith. The House of Wisdom thrived in tenth-century Iraq, but would be blown up by suicide bombers had it existed today. I realized that the maulvis of the mosque during my boyhood had excised important parts of the Islamic story, as though the primacy of the mind was dangerous to those who took religion too literally. There might not be an Islam "out there" in the world willing to accept me, but I could follow my own interpretation, one that made sense to me and was not tied to any mosque or mullah, a faith renewed by a constant questioning of received ideas, especially my own.

On a cold winter day, I found on the library's third floor a biography of the Prophet by a French Jewish intellectual named Maxime Rodinson. In his twenties and thirties, Muhammad would retreat to the mountains to meditate on the injustices he saw around him.

He would found a new religion proclaiming the universal equality of all people—and be nearly killed for it. There was war and violence in Muhammad's story, and in the subsequent history where the caliphs Omar, Osman, and Ali were all assassinated—but that was the nature of politics, of war and peace, and of life itself. For a time, there was not even a single canonical text, the Qu'ran having been compiled during the reign of the third caliph.

It was said that Muhammad was visited by the Angel Jibra'eel in the cave during his first vision, and from his lips poured forth the words of the Qur'an.

Read! the angel had commanded.

But I cannot read, said Muhammad, who was not a god but a human being. The biography of the Prophet said he was unlettered. But it was from Muhammad's lips alone that the Qur'an—a work of world-historic significance—would be revealed. Here was a parable I understood: that the very first miracle of Islam was that an illiterate man was able to read.

I devoured other thinkers and formed my own picture of a complex faith with a complicated history that had been reduced to bloodlust by Western propagandists.

"Muhammad was distinguished by the beauty of his person," wrote one historian. "They applauded his commanding presence, his majestic aspect, his piercing eye, his gracious smile, his flowing beard. . . . His memory was capacious and retentive. . . . He possessed the courage of thought and action." These were not the words of the Qur'an or Hadith, but of Edward Gibbon, author of *The Decline and Fall of the Roman Empire*. So much for the Muhammad-as-warlord narrative.

Brown Boy

After long hours of monkish study, I would walk back to my apartment, the snow crunching underfoot, wondering what else the schools had neglected to mention. I was questioning dogmas, questioning myself, trying to find some harmony within my own restless, divided soul.

13.

Two Faces

A t the start of summer after my second year, I pulled up to
my parents' house with my suitcase in tow. It was evening
and the orange sun peeked behind clouds that looked like shattered glass. The neighborhood looked the same: the same houses
with the same doors, the same bent tree on the neighbor's lawn,
the same porch lights at our house, the same families behind the
same windows.

I had been admitted to study in Paris, at a university called
Sciences Po, or the Institute of Political Studies, for the fall semester.
Most of France's presidents and prime ministers had gone there
and it would be a grand new adventure. Paris instantly took my
mind to the higher things, the worlds of cultivation, elegance, and
intellect. Yet when I went home that summer, rather than a joyous
return, I got a harsh reality check.

My parents and I hadn't spoken in months, and I was not talking
all that much to my brothers, either. There was no bad blood between us. I had just been focused on building my new identity as
a thinker and a student. In that fleeting moment when I stood at
my door, I knew I had changed.

The door swung open and my grandmother stood before me.

"*Beta!*" Dadiye shrieked, a small woman in a bright yellow shalwar kameez. "The white people don't feed you!"

My grandmother blessed my head. I went inside and hugged Amma. My father was sitting at the table with a pink T-shirt and sunglasses—"These go dark in the light"—looking like Robert De Niro.

Amma appeared and put a huge plate of rice and chicken curry on the table, which I ate slowly.

Dada said, "Bloody hydro bill is up again. You guys flush, flush, flush, use too much water. Flush only once or twice. In your mother's village, you know, they don't even have toilets."

"This is not true," Amma said from the stove. "They put the toilets in there now."

I sat at the table, exhausted. I wanted to share with them what I was studying, the thinkers I had befriended, the books I had turned to for counsel, the dreams I was having. But my words failed me.

"Don't study too much philosophy," Dada said. "It will make you go coo-coo."

Amma said, "Finish your food or you will starve."

I told them about Paris, that I would be going at the end of the summer. Amma and Dadiye stayed quiet. My father looked at me with his dark sunglasses.

"How will it *help* you?" he said.

"I need to get more experience of the world," I said. "I haven't seen anything."

"Will it help you get a job?"

I said nothing. I finished my food and could feel the tension roiling through my body. I was unable to explain or express myself to them anymore. My mind hungered for recognition. I wanted to discuss the ideas I was learning, to translate the college world I had seen, but didn't think anyone would understand. I had just gotten home, but I was already prepared to leave.

Later that evening, Amma came into my room.

"Do you still pray?" she asked me. "You know, we must pray."

"Not really, no," I confessed. She had asked me the question in Urdu and I had replied in English.

Amma frowned.

I began to say something in Urdu, something about faith and prayer and how there were multiple ways to know God. But when I tried to explain myself, my Urdu failed me. I could have complex thoughts in English, but my Urdu was still stuck at the level of a child's. I was unable to articulate to my own mother what I felt.

"What is it?" she asked in Urdu.

I stuttered and, frustrated, said, "*Kuch nahin.*" Nothing. I was beginning to lose my mother tongue as I busied myself perfecting my English. Then again, I was back in a world that was my past, and I was out of place. It left me feeling flustered and anxious. Moving between the worlds of college and home disoriented me. That same week, I ran into a girl I went to high school with at the gym. She said, "Holy shit! You talk *totally* different now." She meant it as a compliment—and yet I was left wondering why her surprise made me feel uncomfortable. She had confirmed that I had changed, but I was unsure of what I was becoming. This world of home had silenced me for so long, and now that I had the words to express myself, I still could not articulate what I felt. And if I could not articulate myself to my own mother, then how free was I?

Some part of me was ashamed of this old world. Some part of me wanted to be intelligent and poised like the white people at college. Some part of me wanted to hold on to the past, which was warring with another part that said the past was dead. Part of me resented this world. Part of me loved this world, for this world of home and parents and chicken karahi and Dadiye and quiet blessings was part of me. Here was the vertigo of moving between two universes. You change, return home, and see pieces of yourself scattered around, in old closets, old ghosts, pieces you discarded long ago. The body intuits first what the mind comprehends later: you cannot be two people at once, cannot have two faces—for eventually, both will become strangers.

· · ·

Later that summer, in July, the air was humid, heat bearing down on our heads. I was reading about the arrondissements of Paris and thinking of Hemingway and Fitzgerald and moveable feasts that would satiate my starving intellect. I hadn't had a proper conversation in weeks.

My brother Oz poked his head into my room. He was getting taller and studying business, managing his money well, taking the responsible path of accounting and finance. He was at Queen's now as well, and just as dedicated and organized as he had been as a child. But rarely, if ever, did we communicate, unless it was about errands or logistics. Our father's noncommunicative nature had driven us to a silent competition and each of us had staked out his own territory: me with words, he with numbers.

So I was surprised to see Oz, and I put down my book.

"Hey, listen," he said. "Bunch of us are going camping this week-end. Can you come? Then we'll have enough people for volleyball."

I suspected there was more to this invitation.

"Who's going?"

"You know . . ." He paused, as if holding back. "The Brothers are joining."

I hesitated. I knew his posse—Bilal, Hassan, Nasir, Mustafa, Kareem, Saeed. The first four were religious fundamentalists of various shades who liked to lecture their friends. Kareem and Saeed were more relaxed. Add me and Oz to the latter camp, and we would be evenly split. I thought that if I went, I would be stuck with the boys judging me and lecturing about Allah, all of us crammed together in tents, and me pretending to be religious. The trip did not sound like fun.

"Come on, it'll be fun. You can't just read all day. You gotta get out a bit."

I agreed to go. It was better to be out in the woods than in the desolate suburbs.

A day later, we were driving down the highway toward one of Ontario's grand parks. Outside of Toronto, to the north, there was forestry and nature everywhere—and, of course, Algonquin Park, a hidden gem we took for granted. We couldn't afford a cottage, so we went camping.

In our car sat me, Oz, Saeed, and Kareem. Somebody had pro-cured a bottle of vodka, which was duly hidden in a flask and would have to be kept a secret. The Brothers, meanwhile, were in another car, likely commenting on the eternal punishment for tasting the haram poison. There was a reason Saeed, Kareem, and Oz had nicknamed their four other friends, "The Brothers."

We got to the campsite and set up our tents and started a barbecue. The four Brothers were sitting at one table and my brother and his two friends sat at another. I joined the religious group and we immediately got into a discussion about science.

"You believe in evolution?" Bilal said. "In Darwin's theory?"

I put my burger down. "I don't *believe* in evolution. I accept its description of how we became humans, through natural selection and the filtering of traits over millions of years."

"So you really think we came from monkeys?" Nasir asked, jumping in.

I got frustrated. I had just spent two years in college learning about Erasmus and Copernicus and Galileo and, yes, Darwin. Now these guys were dismissing all of that as foolish. Like *I* was the brainwashed one.

"Humans evolved from primates, yes," I said. "What's wrong with that? Some people still haven't finished evolving."

"So how did life begin?" another boy interjected. "The world has a beginning, a middle, and an end. Allah *subhanawatallah* knows best."

I tried to make a point about how our minds had trouble conceiving infinity. Even though there was a big bang that "created" all of time and space fourteen billion years ago, the next question was always what happened "before" the big bang—but, of course, there was no "before," since there was no "time" and no "matter" prior to that primordial explosion.

"It takes sunlight eight minutes and twenty seconds to reach our eyes," I said. "There are different galaxies around us. Physicists have theories of time travel and black holes. Isn't that more awe-inspiring than . . ." I searched my mind for an example. "More awe-inspiring than Abraham going to slit his son's throat."

"His son was replaced by a goat at the last moment," responded Bilal. "The Qur'an predicted many scientific discoveries."

The conversation was going nowhere, yet I was feeling annoyed at the suggestion that the mysteries of the universe could be limited to a single perspective. For centuries, thinkers of all disciplines and religions had questioned what was out there, beyond our planet, and later, what was here, inside the tiniest particle. I loved to get lost in all these ideas of dark matter, dark energy, the fact that energy could not be altered or destroyed—and then wonder what happened after we died.

Now I was the one in the mood for provocation.

"So," I said to them, cocksure, "you think we adulterers should be stoned?"

Mustafa answered this time, with his whiskers and glasses giving him a holy vibe.

"At the time of the Prophet, peace be upon him, this punishment was a deterrent to keep the community intact. If spouses did not remain loyal, the Muslims would be killed or betrayed. And a guilty verdict required four witnesses to the act itself. The crime isn't necessary to punish in our modern legal system. And anyways, women were punished for adultery in the West until recently."

"Is stoning wrong, though?" I asked.

Bilal-the-Iraqi piped up. "It worked at the time. You know,

during Ramadan in Saudi Arabia, all the owners leave their shops to go pray. Their goods are left out in the open. Why can they do this? Because they know that if someone steals, they will face the harshest penalty."

"Stoning is inhumane," I said.

We went in circles about corporal punishment, cutting off hands, executions.

Nasir, who had a round face, pointed his long fingers at me. "Look at America. They have the death penalty and use it more than any other country. America has probably executed more people than most Muslim countries. And most people they execute are Black."

This started a conversation about American policy, Afghanistan, Pakistan, and Iraq. I tried to make a point about how the problems of Muslim-majority countries could not all be placed at America's feet, that Muslim leaders had to take some responsibility. One of the boys cut me off.

"Ay, man," Nasir shouted at me, "you know Mullah Omar?"

I cringed. "No, I don't *know* the leader of the Taliban. But if I meet him, I'll be sure to give him your number."

"Mullah Omar got rid of opium in Afghanistan."

The discussion was derailed with each one of the boys now taking shots at me. I stuffed a burger in my mouth and joined my brother at the other table with the secular boys Saeed and Kareem.

At this table, the boys were talking happily about women and parties and our upcoming volleyball game. I was agitated and muttering arguments to myself.

"What's good, bro?" Saeed asked. He was Palestinian and one of my brother's oldest friends. "The Brothers interrogate you?"

"Yeah," I said.

Saeed laughed, a happy warrior who accepted what life threw at him and was always in a positive mood. "Did the boys start yelling at you about religion? Don't mess with the Brothers."

"No," I said, exasperated. "We ended up arguing about stoning. Fucking stoning."

They all chuckled, as if we were taking ourselves too seriously. Maybe it was best to leave religion out of friendship, to not even bother arguing about matters that were more emotional than logical. But that was not in my nature.

At that very moment, as if by divine intervention, little Kareem, who had been quiet until now, pulled out a fat joint from his sleeve.

"Wanna do this before the game?" he asked, eyebrows up.

Normally, I would have said no. Then I looked around me, at the trees and bushes and afternoon sun and the sandy beach not too far away, feeling the serenity of a perfect July day. I looked over at the Brothers still arguing at their table.

Slowly, I nodded.

After all that talk about stoning, we would not only defeat the fanatics in a game of volleyball—but would do so while stoned.

Bilal shouted, "Game starts in fifteen minutes!"

The four religious boys huddled together and discussed strategy. Meanwhile, the four of us went behind a bush. The joint was lit, skunk fumes drifting up. When it was passed to me, I drew in a mouthful of smoke and when I exhaled . . . the world receded, reality slowed down, my eyes and lips went dry. And as the smoke

161

cleared, the dust settled like in ancient times, and we were warriors preparing for battle.

Sunlight scorched my eyelids, the lake glistening like diamonds. I could feel each grain of sand in my toes as I walked on the beach.

It was as though we had traveled back in time and now it was the seventh century all over again, the stakes of this game higher than a holy war.

We moved ever so slowly toward the volleyball net.

"You guys okay?" Hassan said. He eyed us suspiciously as the other boys got ready.

No one responded.

I tried not to look at him, giggling to myself. He struck me in that moment as a Bedouin who was about to rally his side in the coming jihad.

"Yeah, yeah, just tired," I said.

"Everyone's tired," he said. "Everyone . . ."

We asked for some time to "rest" after our "walk," and the other boys, thinking we feared losing, gave it to us.

Hassan watched us from the table as we laid our bodies on the beach, unable to move.

"They say they are tired," he said to the other boys, wagging his finger in the air like an auntee. "But it must be something else. No, it *must* be something else."

Soon, the time of the Great Match had arrived.

There were the four of us and the four of them. Bilal-the-Iraqi tied his hair up, and looked to me like the chief of a desert army. The boys had a look of zealous conquest on their faces. They got together and said a prayer.

On our side, we were in a spiritual daze. Sweat dripped from my forehead. We were standing and ready, separated only by a volleyball net.

The dust blew across the expanse of beach. A piercing silence defined the desert around me, and I had the sensation that I was in Arabia in the time of great tumult of centuries past.

Bilal took the first serve. We responded and hit the ball back. Far from decimating our team, the other side quickly realized that we could return their serves and score our own points.

The four religious boys asked for a break. They reassembled to discuss strategy. "These idiots are beating us," Hassan said angrily.

"*Bismillah!*" shouted the server on their end. I hit the ball back at him and it dropped into the sand.

Back and forth we went, neither side conceding. Each time we scored, the boys argued with each other, cursed, and prayed.

The game came down to a final point. The ball arced like a parabola to our end, and Oz leaped forward in slow motion and hit the ball, which went over the net and landed between the boys.

Our side won. The Brothers on the other side were left scratching their heads as if the upstarts had scored a miracle.

Bilal stretched out his fist. "Good game," he said.

I dabbed his fist. "Good game."

It was a metaphorical lesson, a role reversal, a reminder that arrogance in matters of faith was a direct route to being vanquished. Pride always came before the fall. Wasn't that the history of Islam as well, when the believers defeated great armies with humility but lost when they were conceited? I realized, as well, that perhaps I had been too scornful in my own arguments, that all of us were young and overconfident and thinking we knew a lot more than we did. But the Brothers were a lot nicer afterward. We bonded throughout the rest of the day, showing respect for each other's views. What we could not resolve in debate, we seemed to have solved in a game of volleyball.

That night, we all sat around the campfire. Flames flickered in the darkness. Halal marshmallows were roasted. An argument about djinn, those smokeless genies created by Allah, was sparked. I excused myself and went into the woods. The chatter receded behind me. I walked in the darkness with the moon shining between the trees, and I saw the stars above me shimmering. There was a cosmic perspective that was beyond us as mere mortals. How many people had lived before me? Millions, billions? Civilizations, cities, all swept aside and buried under dust. All those humans were capable of the same range of emotions as I, and they had all experienced hope and heartbreak, love and loneliness, determination and defeat. But up there, in the night sky, there was a feeling of eternity, of infinity. I marveled at the silvery stars, these millennia-old implosions looming over me as I stood there in the darkness, observing from the future, still hungering for the universal.

14.

Future Perfect

L ater that summer, my father was still unimpressed by my plans
to go to Paris. He was walking around the house, hair slicked
back like a beret, uttering criticisms under his breath. For a few
weeks, he had just assumed this was a fanciful goal—no one from
around here went to Paris—that would not come to fruition. I
proved him wrong. Now I was spending all my free time reading
the history of France, teaching myself French, and studying maps
of Paris.

My father, irritated, came into my room.

"Why are you going to Paris?" he asked. "You can stay here,
maybe work somewhere. Instead, why not transfer to a university
closer to home?"

"I need to go," I said, getting anxious. "I want to broaden my
world. Europe will be a good experience."

"But how will it *help* you?"

I brooded on the question. For my father, the idea of Paris was
too utopian. It would not translate into a job or into any currency,
so what was the point of going? University was for employment,
not to discover yourself or have adventures, and it didn't matter
what "Europe" or "the West" or "Paris" symbolized.

He grumbled and mumbled.

"You're going to university and making so little money."

"I have a scholarship," I said.

"Your books won't help you pay the bills. And anyways, what do you have to show for yourself after two years of studying?"

I had heard verbal criticisms all my life and tuned out these comments. I also knew that this grumpy, stern-faced treatment was how fathers expressed themselves in our world.

Dada was still angry. "You're going away to Paris. . . . How will we eat?"

I felt the guilt in my throat. I knew he was exaggerating, but still, the idea of creating hardship for my family gnawed at me. Maybe it was better to kill off these dreams before they consumed me. Maybe I should just stay local.

A week later, my father entered my room again. I was surprised to see him.

"My friend," he said, "your uncle Mahmood. Do you remember him?"

I shook my head.

"He has a relative of his, another uncle, who lives in Paris. He said he would take you in until you found a place."

I was elated. Finding somewhere to live in Paris was no simple task, now Dada was coming through for me. I wondered about this uncle, where he lived, what he did, but was too relieved to ask more questions. The uncle was Pakistani; that and his passing familiarity with my father were enough for him to open his door to me. Later, I understood that this uncle was part of that immigrant network of distant family friends who were sprawled across the globe—the uncles and auntees who had migrated to Europe and North America, existing in the background and responding when called upon. This was our social capital: the mechanics, airport workers, cabdrivers, small-shop owners who had arrived a generation before and were now willing to take in a young student from halfway around the world.

It would be easier to find a flat when I was in France. I didn't bother asking where exactly he resided. It didn't matter. I was going to Paris. City of Lights. City of Dreams. Soon I would be taking off on a spaceship, spreading my wings, and flying far away.

· · ·

On my last day at home, my family ate mangoes. It was a special treat that Dada had procured from the local Indian bazaar, and we sat around the table gorging on these yellow fruits with sticky fingers like they were the last mangoes on earth.

We drove to the airport the following evening. Everyone was in a bad mood, the logistics of packing and tickets ruining the atmosphere of goodbye. My father drove in silence. I looked out the window. The leap across the ocean was all too real now.

They had invited other cousins and uncles to the airport, but no one came. Everyone was busy with their own lives. This invitation harkened back to the days of our grandfathers, when a large family farewell accompanied the migrant who was leaving the Indian subcontinent, often for the last time, never to return. The migrant would have boarded a ship bound for England or

North America, and the goodbyes, the tears, the prayers were meant to be final.

Amma embraced me in her arms and would not let go. My grandmother blessed my forehead. But with my father, there was a stoic handshake and a reminder to study diligently in the new land.

"Education is about character," Amma said. "Please, whatever you do, protect your body over there. You don't know that place. You have never gone this far from home."

My father stayed silent.

I assured them everything would be all right. I was always telling them this, but in truth, I had no idea what was waiting for me on the other side of the Atlantic Ocean. I had my suspicions that my romance with Paris might not be exactly as I had dreamt, but it was too late to turn back now.

Reluctantly, I left them there and walked to the gates, looking back every few seconds to wave again, and my grandmother, father, and mother all waving back until their faces disappeared among the rush of heads and bodies.

I boarded the airplane and took my seat in the back. The engines rumbled to life. We took off into the air and circled over the city. I saw the place where I had grown up: the flatlands and thousands of roofs and roads, the curved shoreline in the distance, the cramped spaces, and knew that I was seeing the landscape of my childhood for the first time. I saw the lights twinkling inside the houses and knew that not too long ago I had been a boy in one of those windows, looking out at the strange world and wondering if there might be a place for me in it.

Brown Boy

The plane soared above the gray sea and the houses faded below me, the past dissolving beneath the dark clouds.

I took another breath, recited a silent prayer. The pilot's voice came over the loudspeaker: there was going to be some turbulence up ahead.

IV.
A Colonial Mind

15.

Department 93

I landed at Charles de Gaulle Airport the next morning. It was a hot August day and I rubbed sleep from my eyes, went through customs, and into the large waiting area. I had half hoped that I might be able to see the Eiffel Tower from the airport, but I was mistaken.

Outside, I saw an uncle waiting for me. He had a lanky frame and was wearing dark glasses that fell off the bridge of his nose. In his hands was a sign with my name scribbled on it.

I went toward him, smiling.

"Salaam, *beta*," he said, calling me "son." "I am Uncle Bhutta."

We had never met before, but seeing him, I felt I was encountering a member of my family.

"I work here at CDG," he said as we walked toward his car. "For many years. There's a few of us, Pakistani, Indian, Bangladeshi, we all spend time in the evening together. You make sure to care for your father when he is older. It is a great blessing for a man to care for his parents."

I nodded. It all felt both familiar and strange—familiar because this was a Brown uncle offering his wisdom, strange because I was now in France.

"This one's mine," Uncle Bhutta said, opening the door to a

rusty blue Peugeot. The windshield was cracked. I tried to lift my luggage into the trunk, but Uncle took it from my hands and tossed it in the back in one graceful motion.

"I told you, *na*? I work at CDG."

We drove through the countryside and took a few exits. The long green pastures were bright under the sun. I saw signs, round-abouts, and arrows noting the direction of Paris, but we went in the opposite direction.

Off the highway, we came to a stop. There were chained-up stores with graffiti scrawled over the fronts; large concrete apartment complexes with undefined entrances; and more than a few men just hanging around, kicking a muddy soccer ball. The men were of African and Arab origin and had that aimless look on their faces that I knew so well.

As my observations accumulated, the warning signs went off in my head. We passed a group of French police officers who were speaking to an older Arab man, checking his ID. They got into some sort of argument, and it seemed, for a moment, that one of the officers would draw their weapon. We drove on. I noticed everything: the color changing to gray, the smog in the air, the abandoned lots, the countless men hanging on street corners. It felt like we had driven into the interior of another country.

"Is this Paris?" I naively asked Uncle.

"No," he said warmly, "this is Villepinte. North of Paris. I will show you how to get to the city."

We pulled into a parking lot. I got out of the car and coughed. The weather had changed, the air was murkier. I craned my neck skyward and I saw these colossal apartment buildings that sprawled into the distance—and I knew I was in the projects.

I followed Uncle into the lobby of the building. The door was broken off. There were blue metal lockers inside, half of them dented. A Black woman in a shawl was sitting outside in a lawn chair. Uncle Bhutta said "Salaam" to her and I did the same.

A few young men passed with the same skin color as mine—men originally from the Maghreb or North Africa, I guessed, and I knew that they knew that I was not from around here. Our eyes met for a split second before they carried on.

The elevator opened slowly and Uncle and I got in. It clanked upward, stopped, went up again. Uncle Bhutta dragged one of my suitcases with a broken wheel down a hallway.

Inside his apartment now, I noticed that it resembled the homes of many Muslim families: Arabic calligraphy on the walls, a Pakistani rug, TV playing the local news. He made eggs for me and I sat at the table, tired and jet-lagged.

"You can get a SIM card from this market, it is very easy. I will show you how to get to Paris, which bus you must take and then the train to Gare du Nord. Just be careful at night."

"How far is the city?" I asked.

"It shouldn't be too far," he said. Uncle drew a ring in the air with his finger. "Paris is a circle. We are on the outskirts."

I nodded silently.

"You know, youth here," he said, "they have no jobs, nothing. Police give them trouble. No good school here. Just keep your eyes on your pockets, you will be fine."

I lost my appetite and decided I could sleep away the anxiety I was now feeling.

"*Aram karo*," he said. "When you are ready, you can go to Paris."

In the bedroom, I opened my suitcase and saw what I had forgotten. There was a bag, wrapped in a chador, and I unpacked it and found two mangoes. I was filled with sadness as I began to eat a mango, saving the other one for Uncle. How many times my mother had thought of me when all I was thinking about was the next destination. The next goal. The next objective in the funnel of meritocracy where my value on this earth was to be judged by what I had accomplished. Now I was in the suburbs and I felt sick for home.

I lay back on the bed, realizing I was not living out my idea of Paris anymore but the brutish reality of the Parisian suburbs. It was as though a great trick had been played on me: I had traveled long and far, and yet somehow, found myself involuntarily in the projects of another country. I would have to switch up my attitude. No, I could not be the café-dwelling student of pristine Paris, but would have to default back to self-preservation mode, the boy from Scartown.

My mind raced through a million calculations, how I would have to dress to not stick out, the route I would take to the bus station tomorrow, where I would place my hands, how I would fight back if I was targeted. I would protect my body, pretend to be tough, not act like a foreigner lost in the outskirts of Paris.

• • •

When morning arrived, I woke up hoping I had suffered amnesia and was actually by the Eiffel Tower. I panicked and began zipping up my suitcase as if to rush out. Then I stopped. This suburb was my new reality, at least for now.

I walked to the window. It was gloomy out, a pallor spread across the buildings. The housing compounds looked as grim as ever, these brutalist structures that went on endlessly as if designed to keep residents from leaving. As I soon learned, the word for my new surroundings was *banlieue* and the reason the air was so contaminated was because the *banlieue* had been built in the north and factory exhaust blew in our direction. People here literally breathed in toxins from the City of Lights.

I am in Paris, I repeated to myself.

I've come here for academic study.

I study at Sciences Po.

I'm in the banlieue *by circumstance.*

I will get to Paris soon.

Uncle Bhutta spent his day off from work showing me how to get to Paris, where to purchase an RER card, the path to the Metro that would take me to my university. I spent the day learning about my environment, becoming a student of the suburbs. Before arriving in this other Paris, the word *banlieue* had not been in my vocabulary; in the literature of the city, the suburbs were either neglected, or else, more recently, hyped-up as terrorist breeding grounds. The areas were meant to be avoided and residents of postcard Paris did not come here, nor did the *banlieue* inhabitants go much into the city. In all the stories I read about the Parisian ghettos, there was a single district that was described as the worst of the slums, precisely where I lived now, which was called Seine-Saint-Denis. The suburb was referred to by its postcode, Department 93, or simply, the 93. In the French imagination, these two numbers symbolized all the problems of the country: Muslims, Black people, Arabs, immigrants, crime, violence, and jihad.

When I called local landlords in Paris to inquire about apartments, they all wanted to know where I was currently living. As soon as they heard that I was in Villepinte, in the cursed area code of the 93, they hung up the phone. I would have to find a place to live the old-fashioned way.

The next day, Uncle Bhutta went to work. I slipped on dark sunglasses and a jacket, grabbed my backpack with a handful of euros, and went outside. At the enclosed bus stop, I glanced at myself in the window, saw a dark-skinned man with stubble, his eyes hidden behind dark frames—either trying too hard to blend in, or else blending in seamlessly. Several women in abayas were waiting. Off to the side were young men close to me in age, with bright sneakers and white shirts. One of them had a keffiyeh over his neck. All three took turns watching me. They could not see my eyes, but I was studying them as well. One of them said something to the other in slang I did not recognize. Boarding the bus, I sat at the back and tried to be as inconspicuous as possible, but I had the feeling that I might be followed.

I got off at the stop for the train station and walked briskly to the platform. It was deserted except for me and one other person, a white man with a leather bag. I carried *A Moveable Feast* with me, but already the book seemed to be mocking my new environment. There were no moveable feasts in the *banlieue*. Out here, brothers were starving.

The youths from earlier appeared on the other side of the platform. We exchanged glances and I nervously boarded the train. I could hear my breath in my ears as we clattered forward. I sat down and tried not to think of my current situation. Perhaps I was projecting my fear outward and those young men would not have done me harm. Then again, though we likely shared a religion and might be mistaken for cousins, I was a stranger here, a foreigner, an *étranger*, and knew well enough that no similarities of skin or kin could bridge the chasm between us.

As the train moved, the sight outside my window was like out of a war zone. Broken-down apartments, industrial buildings, abandoned warehouses, graffiti everywhere, and those gigantic brutalist projects. By the time I got closer to the outer limits of Paris, the landscape changed and cleaner buildings and trees came into sight. I had been traveling just under an hour and yet felt I was crossing an invisible border, a frontier blockading the city from the suburbs.

Soon, I was in Saint-Germain des Prés, the luxurious neighborhood where my school was located. The streets were dazzling, and I saw Café de Flore and Les Deux Magots, where Hemingway and Fitzgerald and Joyce drank away their evenings, where James Baldwin had furiously smoked and composed several of the essays in his masterpiece *Notes of a Native Son*. Down one of the roads were high-fashion outlets whose names I could not pronounce; black Mercedes-Benz taxis; wandering American tourists with fanny packs around their large waists. Part of me felt that I had come to the heart of civilization itself. These lights, the smell of espresso, the dog shit on the sidewalk, the chic Parisians: it was like being thrust into another universe.

I ambled toward the Seine, sat down at a café, and watched the river, spending my few euros on a cognac. I took out my journal; when a Muslim family passed by on the street in front of me, I covered the drink with my arms, instinctively not wanting to be judged. I had been reading the Algerian novelist Albert Camus, falling in love with his crisp sentences and the beauty of his art. But the Left Bank, where I sat, was as far from Department 93 as Paris was from Algeria. In my notebook, I wrote: *I am alone in Paris.* I felt torn between my two realities: the bookstores and bars and intellectual life of this Paris and the fog and danger and poverty of Seine-Saint-Denis. What I did not know then was that Paris had been designed to banish *les classes dangereuses*—the dangerous classes—from its center, and that its boulevards and streets and apartments were meant only for the elite. I might read a thousand books and consume the works of Camus and Sartre, but in historical terms, I was part of the masses of undesirables. I was a boy whose immigrant parents had never been to Paris, and I had two selves locked in war. I also knew that I shared more with the residents of the *banlieue* than with anyone around me now. It was this feeling of double vision that made me pause. Romance and disgust mingled within my heart as I finished my drink and felt the burn in my chest.

The real charms of Paris lay not in the Eiffel Tower or the Arc de Triomphe, but in the narrow side streets, the random cafés, the boutique bistros, the used bookshops, the balconies and galleries and the history represented by the buildings. Truth be told, I did not wish to return to Villepinte at all. My sole preoccupation was to move closer to the city center, find an affordable apartment, and begin the life of study in Paris. But every time I idealized Paris now, I remembered what was waiting for me in just a few hours.

All day, I walked across the city, clocking thousands of steps and observing like a *flâneur* the suave French uncles with their scarves and the most beautifully dressed women I had ever seen. Despite my status as an *étudiant* at one of France's premier institutions, I could not shake the feeling of being an outsider.

It was getting dark. The lights were coming on in the cream-colored apartments, in the cafés, and the Eiffel Tower, which I could see from a distance. I gulped down a two-euro espresso and rushed to the train station, hoping to stay out of trouble as I headed back to the periphery, back to the 93.

. . .

At the Metro, I walked underground through a dim tunnel. I was scared moving between shadows, staying within the light, constantly looking behind me.

In the passageway, I witnessed a youth rob someone right in front of my eyes. He was slurring, drunk, and went right up to a middle-aged man, sucker punched him, and tried to steal his wallet. The other man, who looked like an office worker, pushed him back. The youth fell against the wall. He reached into his pocket and brandished a knife. I clutched my backpack straps and ran as fast as I could past him, getting on the train at the last second, panting, terrified.

The train rattled through the darkness. I checked my watch. It would be another hour before I got back to the suburbs. The same ugly fortresses passed me outside. If during the day the projects looked soulless, now they resembled tombstones jutting into the sky. I was traveling back in time, leaving the flirtatious shops of Paris and returning to the outskirts, where the children of France's former colonies lived.

I arrived in the *banlieue* close to midnight. I walked swiftly down the platform and into the station. I saw youth from the neighborhood hanging around—and I was afraid. Though language and geography separated us, we held some things in common: I might say *As-salamu alaykum* and they might even respond in kind. But this was not the time to intellectualize. I knew the rules of the ghetto meant to not stick your head out where you did not belong, not to bring attention to yourself. My senses were on high alert.

Police were at the station that night. Ten, fifteen officers outside in packs, roaming and observing.

"*Attendez!*" an officer shouted. "*Attendez!*"

I froze. The first cop called over to his partners. Two big white French policemen approached, sneering in my face. I remained still.

The bigger officer grabbed my arm and began patting me down, squeezing my biceps, frisking my thighs and groin. He grabbed my belt roughly. I stepped back at the coarse touch of his palms.

The second cop murmured to the first one something about how I wasn't from the 93, and the first cop glanced at me with a look that said, *Why on earth are you here?*

"Villepinte?" I asked in the most nonthreatening voice I could muster.

"Passport!" the first officer said.

I handed it to him. He took a look at my ID and tossed it back at me.

"Go this way," he said in broken English, directing me to the bus.

I walked through the darkness, the slang of French around me, groups of boys posted up, fear gripping my throat. Streetlights flickered. Sounds of static. I felt a sense of disquiet as I moved between the lights, silhouettes of men near me.

No cars were in sight. I thought of what I had in my backpack to use as a weapon: water bottle, pens, hardcover books. I squinted, trying to see clearly. A woman in an abaya approached and this made me feel safe.

"Excuse me . . ." I began.

And then I realized it was the Black woman from Uncle Bhutta's apartment.

"Salaam," I said.

"Salaam," she replied.

The woman seemed unfazed. I asked her apologetically where the bus was supposed to arrive. She pointed to where I was standing.

A few minutes later, the bus came to the stop. I had only thoughts of escape, with a hint of guilt. I was a foreign visitor who could leave. My uncle, the woman by my side, all of the boys—they could not escape.

The bus took me back to Uncle Bhutta's neighborhood. I was vigilant and counted each stop. When we got to the building, I held the door open for the elderly woman and took one last glance at the late-night suburb. The labyrinthine apartment complex loomed over me. None of this was an accident, I thought. None of the feelings this place aroused—of being trapped, deprived, cut off, walled-in—were a mistake.

Standing there in the darkness, I wondered:

What *liberté*?

What *égalité*?

What *fraternité*?

The stench of hashish smoke drifted past me. Dogs barked in the unquiet night. The voices of young men, disembodied, hollered their slang into the endless void.

16.

City of Darkness

In those first weeks, I moved between the suburbs and the Paris Institute of Political Studies like a colonial crossing the barricades to receive an education. The early-morning air in Paris smelled of fresh bread and coffee and I purchased a baguette and strolled into school ready to learn.

Behind the gates of Sciences Po, students were busy discussing the great issues of the day. They smoked hand-rolled cigarettes, book bags slung over their shoulders, and chatted in English and French about the European Union, the migrant "problem," the rise of far-right nationalists. The jokes and laughter were usually about the institute's most famous dropout, Nicolas Sarkozy, *Président de la République française*. European eminences passed through the Institute regularly, pulling up in sleek black cars. The French were always talking big ideas, clothing their beautiful ideals in even more beautiful language.

It was a jarring experience: by day, I was a café-dwelling Sciences Po student taking notes about philosophy and history, walking the streets and staring at Notre-Dame and the many fashionable men and women sitting at small tables outside restaurants, violins playing around me. And by night, I walked with tense muscles through the *banlieue*, a double existence that was wearing me down.

I was still struggling to find a place in Paris on a tight budget, when I was introduced to a landlady by a student at Sciences Po. She was a robustly built French lady named Madame Marie-Claude, and after some convincing she rented me an apartment. It was at Square du Croisic, by Boulevard des Invalides and Rue de Sèvres.

A large, sweating Madame Marie-Claude, fanning herself with a paper, met me at the gated entrance after class one day. All I could think about was not being too late—or else I'd be going back to the *banlieue* in the dark.

"*Ç'est trop chaud!*" she shouted. "*Alors! Je te montre.*"

My French was not good, but I thought I understood her as she led me into the building. Her English was so poor that we barely could communicate, resorting at times to sign language and slow yelling.

We walked up five flights of stone stairs. Madame Marie-Claude was breathing heavily; so was I. When we got to the top floor, I realized that those big windows were for the rooms below us. We were in a hallway with a dark green carpet, dusty and dirty, the air smelling of smoke.

Madame brought me to a door and opened it.

"*Voilà,*" she said.

I looked about the room in a state of disbelief. It was the size of a tiny attic. There was a narrow entrance. A small desk pressed against the kitchen, which consisted of a rusting hot plate. And then the bed. The ceiling slanted downward so that it was only a foot from where my head would rest. I later learned that the same nineteenth-century man who destroyed and rebuilt the city, Baron Haussmann, had also designed the apartments so that the nobles lived in the lower quarters and the servants in these garrets at the top.

A small window with bars looked out onto the city. The whole room, taken together, was not more than a hundred square feet. It felt like a closet.

"*La chambre de bonne*," she said.

A maid's room, a room of my own.

I looked around again. It was either this, or the 93.

"I'll take it," I said.

And so began my voyage into the other Paris.

· · ·

Paris was an unforgiving city, a jealous lover who guarded her intimate secrets from outsiders.

During my first days, I had met three young men: Max from England; Philip from Germany; and Matthew from Montreal. We formed a motley crew, going to parties and lectures together, cracking jokes. They were white, I was not, but in the early days of my Paris romance there were no color lines I wanted to see. Though Matthew might complain about how the Parisians mocked his Quebecois accent, I found that each of them felt more at ease in Paris, whether talking to random people, gossiping with students, or introducing themselves to French women.

"*Enchanté*," Max had said to a new friend.

Enchanté, I repeated to myself quietly, standing behind him.

My learning gap was larger, but I got some important shortcuts by being friends with Max, Philip, and Matthew. I had studied French for one year in college, and one year in high school, and from where I stood now I saw how ignorant I had been. In my old neighborhood, there was no point in learning French. When would I ever speak to a French person?

With these friends, I saw the Eiffel Tower, marveling at its metal structure, though the hagglers and stragglers around the tower made the visit uncomfortable. I saw Versailles, amazed at the opulence of King Louis XIV. The golden palace was grotesque in its riches, gold everywhere, the gardens glowing in symmetry. When we walked through the king's bedroom with its smaller-than-anticipated bed—"That's where Marie Antoinette and King Louis shagged," said Philip—I wondered if the royals had been nervous as the mobs made their way from Paris.

At the Louvre, I stood on the floor in front of the *Mona Lisa*. The world's most impressive painting was less impressive up close behind its glass shield. A thousand cameras and heels clicked as I walked upstairs for what I really wanted to see: the Code of Hammurabi. A black stele totem, this was the very first body of written laws in recorded human history. The Code was dated to 1700 BCE. It enshrined that oldest of unwritten laws—*lex talionis*, an eye for an eye, a law the young men of the *banlieue* knew well. A law that I had grown up on.

A couple weeks later, we attended a party in a crowded loft in the fifteenth arrondissement, and I stood nervously and watched the others interact, trying to mimic them, mime them, my broken French sputtering into clear English, making small talk, not revealing a single detail about my past. I was still so ashamed of my own difference from these people and their effortless movements that I'd rather stay silent than risk saying the wrong thing.

After a few drinks, I was accosted by a chain-smoking man named Guillaume. He had dark hair and a large forehead, with the lined face of a Parisian intellectual. We had been talking about secularism when the subject of France came up.

"Multiculturalism does not work," he said. "Do you know the *laïcité*?"

"I believe so," I said, understating my own knowledge. In fact, I had taken multiple courses on political theory and had tried to understand the full breadth of the term.

"The *laï-ci-té*," he said, enunciating it for me.

I knew the word, yes. The uniquely French concept of absolute removal of religion from a neutral public space. In Anglo-America, secularism meant protecting both the state and the individual, and it would have been unconstitutional for the government to tell a Jew not to wear a yarmulke or a Muslim woman not to wear the hijab. The freedom of religion and the secularism of the state were balanced. *Laïcité* in France, begun as a check on the all-powerful Catholic Church, was how the state overpowered religion, eradicated its display, though Catholicism still played a central role in French culture. *Laïcité* was more than just a rule; it was a test of assimilation.

"*Laïcité*," Guillaume said, "should apply to everyone, and the immigrants do not wish to follow this."

I nodded along.

"If you have come here, you must become French."

I nodded again. I tried to say something about Muslims being no different than others, but the streets of the *banlieue* flashed before my eyes and I knew I would be lying. Muslims—and Arabs and Black people—*were* treated differently in France and considered foreign. The country didn't even collect racial or ethnic data because everyone was supposed to be equal. Yet from the moment that I stepped foot in Paris, it was clear to me that this equality was based on a fiction. I wondered whether the term *laïcité* was now used as a weapon against those who looked different. And I hid the fact that my mother wore the hijab from my new friends. Though I wished to easily integrate and assimilate, if I was forced to choose between *laïcité* and my mother, I hope I would have chosen my mother.

When Guillaume turned away, I put my drink on the table and quietly slipped out the door, disappearing into the Paris night.

· · ·

As the weather darkened that fall, the hailstorms beat against my window. I sat in bed in my attic, smoking a cigarillo and reading Albert Camus.

France no longer ruled its colonies, but the people of the colonies had come to France; the colonies were reconstituted in the suburbs to the northeast and among the Arabs and Black people of Paris itself. I thought of how, twenty years after Marshal Pétain's government in Vichy collaborated with the Nazis to send Jews to the death camps, France was fighting to keep Algerians in bondage. The scale of France's violence in Algeria was horrendous. French officers tortured thousands of Algerians on an industrial scale. Over a million Algerians were slaughtered in a senseless colonial war. In those days, on the streets of Paris, Arabs were thrown into the Seine in broad daylight.

Albert Camus, born in Algeria, was torn about the plunder of his homeland. I asked myself: Did pronouncing the noblest ideals blind people to the evil within themselves? Violence begat more violence. France had desecrated Algeria, murdering and maiming the inhabitants. The children of Paris's suburbs today, like the grandchildren of Paris's colonies yesterday, were accustomed to such violence.

Camus had once captured the quandary of existence, the need to find meaning as we choose to live on. "There is but one true serious philosophical problem, and that is suicide," wrote Camus. When I walked the streets of Paris, I tried to trace this history backward. From the standpoint of the colonized, there was but one true *political* problem—and it was homicide. Kill us or be killed. Cage us or be caged. Conquer us or be conquered. Colonize us or be colonized yourself. Perhaps this is what the West was truly afraid of: that what they had done to others would now be done to them.

Paris was growing dark. The city was isolating me. The slush of cars, the Parisians elbowing others as they walked, the retreat into golden apartments. Gone was the romance of the summer. I saw more French soldiers with machine guns, keeping a watchful eye on the citizenry.

With the change in weather, and the rain at all hours, my spirits started to sink. I stayed in my attic room more and more and watched the darkening streets. Paris was pulling me deeper into her embrace, undressing my emotions, removing my mask.

I could feel another disturbance knocking at my door.

...

One day that November, I did not get up from bed.

My whole body felt heavy, like I had gained a hundred pounds overnight. I don't know what came over me, but I suddenly became indifferent to my studies. What was the point of all this studying? I wondered. What did academics achieve anyway? Even if I worked hard and went to a good law school in America, I could not escape my family's judgments, the verdicts of the wider world, or the fact that I felt so terribly, sickeningly alone.

I had an inner voice that whispered to me at my lowest moment, *You're nothing.* An amalgam of all the critical voices I met who suggested that no matter what I did, I would forever remain an illiterate Paki. The love had evaporated from my life and I began to reject all the external markers of success.

Online, I saw pictures of friends enjoying their time at the college I had left. I heard Sheela had moved on to a man from her "culture," who had more money. My loneliness engulfed me and my mind started to break down. It looked like four o'clock in the morning outside at all hours—and felt like four o'clock in the morning within my soul.

Soon, I stopped going to class altogether. I stopped taking care of how I looked, sleeping in until the late afternoon, with the ceiling a few inches from my face. A part of me was wilting, dying inside, and I was turning my back on all the dreams I had once imagined. Dread should have filled my chest, for I knew that the rule at Sciences Po was that three unexcused absences meant an automatic fail in the class. Still, I did not care. The next thing

I knew, I hardly even wanted to read anymore. Books, once my greatest joy, now became tasteless and sterile.

I defaulted on one class, then another, then another. I failed, failed, failed. And rather than panicking at the prospect of ruining my future so early on, I couldn't even force myself to move. My spirit, once so turbulent and propulsive, had come to a grinding halt. My life became this attic, this desk, this tiny window. I had become a prisoner of my own distorted mind.

Friends from the Paris Institute asked where I had been. I could not respond to them without being paralyzed by shame. My father called me and asked how I was doing and I lied and said I was busy with school. Uncle Bhutta even drove from the suburbs to my apartment on Eid and waited outside, but I did not know he was there. I did not even realize it was Eid. It did not matter anymore. I was sunk deep into the abyss.

The past had finally overwhelmed my future. My education had been my raison d'être, and now I didn't have the motivation to look at even a single page. I had fallen through an invisible trapdoor. I had lost the one thing I was most proud of: my inspiration to learn.

In my readings of Albert Camus, I found these words in his journal: "Being able to live alone in one room in Paris for a year teaches a man more than a hundred literary salons and forty years' experience of 'Parisian life.' It is a hard, terrible, and sometimes agonizing experience, and always on the verge of madness." At the time, I dared not use the word *depression*, but that was the ailment torturing me from within, mocking me, refusing to let go.

It was useless to seek out causes of this pain, but later I did try to piece together the puzzle. Perhaps I was predisposed to depression, as many people are, but my circumstances contributed to the burden: the toll of living a double life was too severe. One too many slights, one too many harsh realizations left me without hope. Part of it was all that internalized hatred, the double consciousness of being insufficient in my own world while being an imitator and assimilator in the white world. I woke up one day and recognized all the lies I had been told. Exclusion can be felt in the body, in the tendons and cartilage and the roughened skin, in the arteries and veins, in the lungs and the quickening heartbeat and the absence of words—but it was endured in the mind.

Years later, I read the letters between the writer V. S. Naipaul and his father, who was a struggling journalist in impoverished Trinidad. When Naipaul was a schoolboy at Oxford in the 1950s, he suffered a mental breakdown. His father, one year before his own untimely death, wrote a letter to his son. "Do not be afraid. . . . You see, my dear Vido, we are not just a mass of flesh and bone. We are also what our ideas have made us." I was the sum of all the ideas I had of myself, of all the ideas the white world had of me. These ideas could be poison, mental cyanide for my self-worth. And what was truly frightening was that a moment could arrive in anyone's life when they woke up one day, looked in the mirror, and were unable to recognize who—or what—they saw. The number of brown-skinned people who committed suicide was too large to count—and in our culture, "mental health" didn't even exist.

For days, I did not leave my room. I smoked tobacco—a terrible habit I had picked up in Paris—and listened to J. Cole and John Coltrane, with some Chopin thrown in for good measure, my spirit finding elevation one or two minutes a day. If I was lucky, I read a single page. Otherwise, life was entombed in silence.

Late one night, sitting on the edge of my bed, I thought of my family, how I was letting everyone down. Those boys who had sneered at my reading would be proven right. And the sacrifices of my immigrant parents. I thought of my grandmother, who had said to me, "I pray that you become all that I imagine you to be." Guilt tormented me and I put my face into my hands.

No matter what I did, Paris brought me right back into myself, showing me what I had kept hidden, suppressed.

Silence—a long, suffocating silence. The dam broke a minute later.

I crashed down on my bed, and for the first time in a long time, I cried. Cried for the life I had lost, for how I had failed to be strong in the face of difficulty, cried for the future that would not exist. I cried for my mother and father, the hopes I had squandered.

I was nakedly exposed before the world—and the world had told me I was no good.

What would I do now? Where would I go?

17.

Nocturne

The thing about feeling like you've already died is that a day comes when you feel ready to live. It doesn't happen all at once, and for some people it might take years, but arrive it does, the way sunlight peeks out of the clouds after the thunder and rain have passed. Once I accepted that my mind was no longer cooperating with my goals, I began to force myself to get out of bed, take a shower, walk down the five flights of stairs, and head to the gym. I could not think my way out of my problems.

The way to get out of the mind was to get back into the body, in the physical sensations of training and walking, in the movement of arms and legs, the counting of breaths. This became an essential part of my routine: no matter how awful I felt or how little I had done during the day, walking to the gym and working out became sacred activities. Naturally, I met other men there and we spoke casually about exercises and sets, and this, too, brought a measure of relief. After the evening's session, I forced myself to go to Shakespeare and Company, the famous bookshop, and took two or three books off the shelf and found a quiet spot to read. Simply being in the presence of other people seeking out books in such a luminous space made me feel less alone.

Then I walked slowly back to my attic, telling myself to listen to this pain, to pay attention to what was happening inside of me, the signals the pain was sending, not to suppress my emotions or try to annihilate them with the opiates of external achievement. I was raised in a culture where men did not have feelings, everything was held inside, and when I finally accepted that it was normal to feel sad, to be lost in grief, I began to heal. I decided I would cut my studies in Paris short and return home to finish college.

In early December, after I had already booked my ticket home, something remarkable happened. I was walking through the streets of Paris at night after the gym when I felt a tap on my shoulder.

I turned around. Standing before me was a tall man with warm eyes and the relaxed demeanor of an American.

"You dropped this," he said, handing me my wallet.

"Oh," I said, surprised. "Thank you."

He was racially ambiguous with a shaved head and a light beard. He looked like an artist, someone you might encounter at a poetry reading or a jazz club.

"I'm Tom, by the way. Mind if I walk with you?"

"Not at all," I said, heartened to make a friend.

"You been in Paris long?"

"About five months," I said.

"Like it here?"

I thought of lying to him, but decided to be honest. "Actually, I've been having a hard time here."

Tom threw his head back in laughter. It was a laugh of recognition, as though I need not say any more.

"Shit, Paris'll do that to you, man. She'll give you a great time for a while, but then break your heart sooner than you realize."

We walked to Odéon station. Tom was from Miami, had come to Sciences Po as a graduate student, and now was making a living in Paris working random jobs, involved in different artistic communities, and always ready for a good time. We talked a bit about our families, the latest news in hip-hop, how Tom had recently broken up with his girlfriend and was feeling his own loss. We bonded over our shared love of music, of certain books neither of us had finished, and being North Americans in Paris.

"Don't worry," he said, slapping my back. "I'll show you another side to the city."

I went home feeling the tinge of happiness. My friend knew Paris well and I wanted to see his version of this chaotic city. That Friday, I dressed in a black shirt and met Tom close to the Champs-Élysées, not on the main boulevard but one of the side streets. There were luxury cars parked outside. Tom was on the phone, a beanie cap on his head, talking rapidly in French.

"My man," he said, giving me props. "Let's roll."

He led me to a building with a nondescript black door.

"This is the spot."

The bouncer, a huge Black man in a camel-hair coat, gave me a suspicious look. But as soon as Tom said, "He's with me," the same giant extended a fist as if we were brothers.

We walked through the iron door and down a flight of stairs and then came upon a second door, where a woman was waiting. Tom said a few words and she smiled and opened the door. I took a step inside and the door closed behind us.

It was like the scenes in my eyelids went from black-and-white to deep purples and blues. Dim lights shone over plush couches, suede chairs, fancily dressed patrons, drinking and smoking. Some were in suits, others dressed casually, still others looking like they had gotten off a film set. It was as though I had stepped through a wormhole and gone back to the Paris of the 1920s.

I followed Tom through the hazy room, noticing the elegant French women and the stylish French men. Everyone was older. I stood in the corner wondering how I had gotten here. As it turned out, Tom was close friends with all the barmen, concierges, valets, reservation takers, bouncers, security guards in the city: the men who protected this world from intruders and tourists.

"That's the top actress in Paris," Tom said, pointing out a woman with auburn hair. He pointed out a man in a dark suit with a jealous look on his face. "That's her ex-lover." He noted another woman in a black dress. "That's the biggest up-and-coming painter in the city.

"Come on," Tom said. "I'll introduce you."

I was terrified. "I'm good here, you go without me."

"Just come on," he said.

Tom walked right up to the group. I followed behind. When he said hello, they all looked at me. Tom introduced me in French. I politely said my *enchanté* and afterward, the men and women raised their glasses to the newcomer in their circle.

It was an alternative universe, hidden, one where I was viewed as an individual without the baggage of my past. I wanted this freedom to last, even if it was an illusion of the night. I leaned against the wall, sipped a stiff drink, observed the freewheeling artists and intellectuals with their faces shining under the lights. I was drawn to this world, not because of its wealth, but because ideas and freedom were in the air. The feeling of creation, of things about to be drawn, painted, written, recorded—art that might one day shake the conscience of others. For a few moments, I was stunned, enthralled, and forgot that I was almost out of money.

The next week, Tom took me to another gathering, this one at Saint-Germain-des-Prés, with many more Black artists than I had seen until now. The men and women were gorgeous, and they spoke with an authority that revealed they had broken out of the narrow shackles that life had placed on them. They had defined their own existences. Once more I saw these free-floating virtuosos who breathed new life into my dreams. They asked me not what tribe I belonged to or where I went to school but what I wished to create out of my life. Tom was like that, too, comfortable in his own skin. It was an aspiration of mine to be as free as these people dancing and speaking, especially when the morning arrived.

I saw how, beneath the surface of gilded Paris, other conversations were happening in other rooms. We were not a lost generation at all, but were a generation struggling with love, fighting against the machines of capitalism and technology, watching as old worlds fell away and new ones waited to take their place, each one of us seeking to wring from this precious life some meaning that had eluded us until now.

After a few weeks of seeing the glitz of Paris, I knew it was time to leave. Just when the party was getting started, but that was my fate. I would have to work harder, work quietly, work in the darkness.

On my last day, I said goodbye to Tom.

"You take care and get back on track, all right?" he said, giving me a hug.

I wished I'd had more words than "Thank you." Tom was the guardian angel who touched my shoulder one evening and pulled me out of the hole into which I had fallen. What Tom had given me was friendship when I needed it most, and in a way, he had saved my life. Maybe that's what all of us misfits craved most: to be seen and heard for who we were.

As the snow fell over Paris and the Christmas lights went up along the Champs-Élysées, I accepted my academic failings. There was something about failing that allowed me to let go. Since the last year of high school, I had been manically determined to get the top grades, educate myself, and prepare for law school: become somebody other than the person envisioned by my old surroundings. I was so insecure about my intellectual abilities that I had to keep proving myself at higher levels. Such tunnel vision had blinded me to life. Failure was teaching me how to be gentle, how to accept my vulnerabilities, how to be honest and compassionate with myself—especially when no one was around. The road to any success, I was learning, was paved with a thousand failures.

On my last night in Paris, I finally went to Café de Flore. I sat alone in the empty café, warming myself with tea and writing. Despite my failings, I was still here, breathing. I still had the desire to hustle, knowledge in my head, immigrant blood in my veins. Still had that greatest of all gifts of those born to immigrant parents: the refusal to be extinguished.

I might have failed, but I would not say I was a failure. I might have been derailed, but I would not be defeated. Not yet, anyway.

18.

Home Rule

I spent the next year with my head down and working hard. I reconnected with friends and met new professors. Since I had suffered a setback, I felt like I had nothing to lose, so I was willing to walk right into the office of a professor whose work interested me—on foreign policy or international affairs—and introduce myself. I was willing to pursue new angles in my papers that might not be the safest choices but would make for an interesting exploration. Having tasted the bitter swill of depression, I had begun to lose my hesitation.

I enrolled in a course on US foreign policy. It was taught by an American named David Haglund, who was an old-fashioned professor, talking freely and without notes, making jokes. He had gray hair, reddened cheeks, the sort of man who might read the memoirs of a nineteenth-century statesman for fun on a Friday evening.

"Understand history," he told me in his office. "It isn't finished yet, whatever Professor Fukuyama might say." He was referring to Francis Fukuyama's much-quoted work, *The End of History and the Last Man*, published during the waning days of the Cold War, predicting that liberal institutions were the end point of history.

Professor Haglund took me under his wing and I wrote a thesis for him on Obama's foreign policy. He advised me on the ways of the American elite, how they valued second and third degrees and loved the word *merit* above all others. Haglund became like a father to me and was always ready to dispense advice or simply listen to the arguments about foreign affairs that I was having with myself.

International affairs had always been the subject that fascinated me the most: the idea that we were all connected, that every government pursued its own self-interest, and that our lives were shaped by what governments did abroad as much as what they did at home. Raised in a Pakistani immigrant household, I was used to international politics being discussed with fervor, the events in Afghanistan and Pakistan and India and China deliberated as if they were happening next door.

I mapped out how to make my mark in the world of international affairs. I would become a foreign policy advisor, I told myself. First, I would apply to England for a master's degree. I wanted to go to the country that had ruled over the lands where my grandparents once lived. It was out of Great Britain's empire that Canada and America both emerged, out of that nation's legal system that the common law had evolved. Studying in England, I believed, would be a triumph over my failures in Paris. Perhaps there was something of a colonial in me wishing to return to that once-imperial nation. Perhaps it was another hurdle to clear in my insecure psyche. After England, I reasoned, I would try for one of the great law schools in America, institutions that molded the leadership class of America. I would try to understand the language of the law, which was the language of power, and power, I was learning in my studies, was how change actually happened in the real world.

The plan had been set and could not be disturbed now. Though I needed these advanced degrees to prove myself, I was also doing what many minorities did when faced with the punishing standards of meritocracy: over-credentialize ourselves in the hopes that we could look the powerful white man in the eye one day, and say, *Now you can't question my intelligence.*

Once the fantasy of England took hold of me, I grabbed on to it and lived with a new sense of purpose. I applied to both Oxford and Cambridge—those great bastions of British education—and sought out every scholarship for which I was eligible. Why Oxbridge? They were the top schools for international relations, with histories going back a thousand years. But it was extortionately expensive and there was no way my family could afford it. So I went out to win some funding.

After failing to get a scholarship for Oxford, I set my sights on the second-oldest university in England. Cecil Rhodes, the diamond merchant and colonialist, could keep his blood money. I would get myself to Cambridge.

• • •

It was a frenzied time: working hard at college, working hard to read more about history. Osama bin Laden had been killed earlier in the year in Pakistan, and once more there were questions about what the government of Pakistan knew in advance. In my family, it became a running punch line: *Obama killed Osama.* I spent countless evenings arguing with uncles about Afghanistan, Pakistan, and as it was then known, in reductive language, "Af-Pak." I believed in the mission of the United States and allies to rout out the Taliban and create a democracy in Afghanistan. The thorn in my side was Pakistan, which was funding the Taliban and supporting attacks on US and coalition forces. Pakistan's intelligence agency, the ISI, was playing its own double game next door, and more innocent Pakistanis were dying because of blowback.

My uncle Nadeem, who had lived in New York, pushed back at my arguments. He was bald with a goatee and high cheekbones.

"America will withdraw and wipe its hands of Afghanistan as soon as it's convenient. Just like they did in the 1980s," he said.

"They won't," I said. "No way they'll let the Taliban win. Otherwise, what's the point of fighting in Afghanistan? If Pakistan wasn't funding the Taliban, there would be more stability. And the US has given how many billions to Pakistan since 9/11?"

Nadeem sat up. "Let me put it to you this way, Omer," he said. "America is the uncle that pays for your college but molests you along the way. You might get a great education, but you'll be traumatized for life."

I tried arguing with his logic, but it was clear that he and the other Pakistani uncles just didn't see the world the same way. They viewed America as an empire pursuing short-term interests in the region—not for twenty years, but forty years, ever since the Soviet invasion of Afghanistan in 1979. They glossed over Pakistan's own hand in creating the Taliban. Sometimes, our debates turned into loud, angry affairs, as I was accused of being a stooge for America's military aims, and I accused them of blaming all their problems on the West.

Still, I resisted the social pressures around me and kept to my vision of working in foreign policy. I had sent in my application to Cambridge, prayed I would get a scholarship, and went home for the holidays.

• • •

Finishing up my college degree was my sole priority now. I took on extra courses, made up for the credits I had lost in Paris, slept little, and was studying and reading for hours at a time.

Shortly after the new year, while I was visiting home, my father's younger sister, Maliha, died suddenly in her sleep. She was the one we called *baji*, or sister; the one who scolded me with love and always told me I should take care of my mother. She was the female version of my father. The death happened so suddenly that the family was reduced to silence. All my father could say was that heart attacks and aneurysms and blood clots took our people in the dead of night, and then it was all over. I wondered how many of our auntees and uncles and parents dropped dead too young due to causes that could have been prevented. Even Baji and Dada's father, my paternal grandfather, whom I never met, died of a heart attack in the prime of his life.

We did not share our secrets or confide our sorrows, just prayed and plowed on with strength—until our bodies shut down.

"Focus on your studies," Dada said. "Don't let this derail you."

But I already knew that's what I would do, subdue all my feelings and not try to make sense of the loss, or the fact that my grand-mother was burying her only daughter. Some things had to be left unsaid. I was an expert at going ice cold and dissociating from my surroundings. Work became my coping mechanism again, my survival and purpose.

"Our stories," Amma said to me, "have already been written from above. But we must live them through the end."

. . .

In February, the coldest month, I found a letter waiting for me. I pushed myself off the chair and stood up and stared at the words. I had been accepted to Cambridge University with a scholarship. And my first thought was *There must be a mistake.* But there was none.

I walked downstairs, opened the door without my jacket, and just breathed in the frozen air for a second. I would remember how fleeting the moment of acceptance felt, how I wished to have cherished it longer, since right away I was already calculating finances, the cost of plane tickets, the many small costs that added up and that children of working-class parents could not afford to overlook.

A couple of months later, in the spring, I broke the news to my family. When I told them, my father, mother, and grandmother were seated around the table having tea.

"I got into Cambridge," I said.

Dadiye gave a confused stare. "*Hein?* Oggs-ford?"

"Cambridge," I said.

In Urdu, she asked, "Cambridge is part of Oggs-ford?"

My father knew Cambridge and said, "Good."

Like Dadiye, Amma did not know Cambridge, but both pretended to understand what I had said.

"It's a good university," I explained, adding gratuitously, "better than Oxford."

"Oggsford . . ." Dadiye said, as if recalling a fond memory. "My older brother studied there."

I was puzzled, but my father explained later that by Oxford she actually meant London.

From the kitchen I walked to the living room. I looked upon the pictures of the men from the past. There was my grandmother, on her wedding day, sitting with a handsome man with impeccable hair: Shuaib Aziz, my paternal grandfather, who was considered one of the most respected men of his community in Lahore. There was the photograph of a dark and wizened man, Amma's father, from their village in Murree, who worked to build things with his hands. And there was the doctor, Dadiye's brother, with a bright face and a thick white mustache, who had become a psychiatrist in London, nearly lost his mind, married a white woman, and then went back to the newly created state of Pakistan and opened up a mental hospital. ("He was both a patient and a doctor there," my father noted dryly.)

I had only met my mother's parents. And, of course, Dadiye had always lived with us. The rest of the elders had been missing from my life. Most had passed away; some were in Pakistan. I wondered what it must have been like for my great-uncle to travel from colonial India to England, to study medicine in a society that ruled over him and his people. Did he try to fit in like me? Did he showcase his difference? Was he a loyal servant of the Crown, or a quiet rebel? Perhaps he was a mix of all these at once: a man grateful for the opportunities of education, the proximity to the center, while also aware that he was still a colonial subject.

I looked from the black-and-white photographs back to my

parents and grandmother, who were about to launch into an argument about Islam and money. The fact that the news hardly struck a chord at home now did not matter. I was on the path to building an even stronger intellect and testing myself at even higher levels.

The birds sang early that February, but I sensed that Cambridge would be another mazelike labyrinth, a world with trapdoors and escape hatches that I would have to avoid.

• • •

That June, I graduated from college. My parents and grandmother were there, proud and beaming, all of them wearing sunglasses and bright colors. Not only did I become the first person in my family to graduate from college in the West, but I had also won the gold medal for my class. I had shown up barely able to write and far behind everyone around me. And I was leaving with new skills, new words, new worlds of knowledge. But I also knew I had more to experience and witness.

I stayed in town that night to celebrate with my friends. Ten of us walked together to the bar. It was a gorgeous evening and I felt alive, young, and still innocent—I was on my way to being educated and had much to be thankful for. The world had not yet destroyed our idealism, and we felt the hope of the newly graduated.

When we entered the dimly lit tavern, something was off. I saw the sweaty backs, the baseball caps, the goatees, the pints of beer, the white men who watched us.

We got a table off to the side, five men and five women. I went to use the bathroom.

Brown Boy

When I returned to the table a few moments later, I saw that the guys had gone to the bar. The girls were looking at each other with discomfort. A large whale of a man was trying to talk to them. His white shirt clung to his love handles. His eyes, when I saw them, were fixed on Melissa, who was clearly not interested.

"Oh! There you are," Melissa said as I approached. "We were just talking about grad school. . . ."

I looked from their faces to the man standing right by me now. He wasn't getting the message, so obvious to me, that the women didn't want to talk with him. It was infuriating; had I been in his position, I would have run away and changed my game by now. But the bulky man just stood there, as if we owed him our attention.

Melissa tried to make small talk with me.

The man interrupted: "You here to take my girl away?"

I was irritated by him now. "She's not *your* girl." But I thought, better to be respectful so he would leave us alone. "Listen, man, we're just here to have a few drinks, then we're going back to campus."

"Who the hell are you?" he shouted.

Spittle came from his lips. I could smell beer on his breath. He stretched himself tall and his stomach stuck out of the bottom of his shirt.

"*This* is your friend?" He pointed at me in front of the women.

I stood there, stunned.

"I ain't going nowhere," the man said. "But if you got a problem with me . . ." He looked around the bar, back to the stools, where several other men were staring at us. "I got about six ex-military guys who might have something to say."

211

Omer Aziz

I was scared but could not show it. I knew what such white men could do.

"You should mind your own business," I said.

The big white man smirked. "You know," he said, "I done three tours of duty. Been to Afghanistan. You know what I used to call your people?"

He leaned in and whispered, "Target practice."

Rage tore through me. I clenched my fists, stepped forward in calm fury.

The man took a step back and then I knew I had him, had called this bully's bluff. When the other men in our group showed up, he seemed less sure of himself.

The whale looked around at his friends, who didn't budge.

"Naw," he said, "we don't want no problems tonight," and then waddled away back to his table.

The women talked about how they were always harassed. More drinks were ordered, and everyone went downstairs to dance.

"I'm heading out," I told them. I left the bar and walked down the summer college streets. This encounter shook me. How casually the words came off his lips. *Target practice.* And to think that just hours before I had graduated and been with my parents.

I was walking faster now, cursing. Hand in my pocket, I touched the gold medal in my jeans. I seethed, feet moving, and I wanted revenge.

To hell with being twice as good! To hell with being twice as polite! To hell with being *gracious* to people who would do me harm. What had *being nice* ever gotten me but the ridicule of the white world?

Brown Boy

Indignant with rage, I walked and cursed until I ran out of energy.

The clock ticked with empty urgency, down to the last minute, and a flash of a few months later: the summer was ending and I was heading to the airport once again, crossing the ocean, and flying to the land of tea and imperialism.

19.

While England Slept

No matter the allure of France, I had one thing going for me in England and that was my language. Though I had spoken Urdu with my grandmother and mother, my thoughts were in English and I prided myself on having improved my vocabulary over the years. England, and the English, were also in my bloodstream: by birth I was a child of British North America, and by roots a grandchild of British India. No longer simply a boy from the colonies, I was entering a Britain where Brown and Black people from the former empire had made their home for generations.

Dusk was setting in as I got off the bus in Cambridge. Like many students new to the town, I was struck by the architectural wonders: the grand steeples of King's College Chapel, a magnificent sight, and the narrow walkways, the shops and shopkeepers, a thousand bicycle bells ringing. I heard the sounds of different British accents, already trying to match accent to social class, which I had read was a major differentiator on this island. I walked down the street and gathered myself at the symbols of history around me: it was here, at King's College, where John Maynard Keynes had revolutionized the field of economics, where the great debates about rebuilding the world economy had taken place after the First

World War. Dragging my suitcase behind me, I found my way to Trinity College.

The University of Cambridge was bigger in real life than even in my imagination. At Trinity College, I went up to the gates and saw a glorious courtyard. The tower seemed to evoke all the greatness of Cambridge's past, and the clocks clanged at the hour. Sir Isaac Newtown had walked through this courtyard, as had Bertrand Russell, the old philosopher probably smoking his pipe and discussing how to avert nuclear war. Time itself felt dilated here, as though every nook and sidewalk and grand college entrance led to a portal into the past. There was an inner rhythm to Cambridge, in the stones and arches and bridges, the black-gowned students, that echoed through the ages.

It occurred to me while standing at Trinity College that Jawaharlal Nehru, the first prime minister of independent India, had also attended Cambridge and would have been in this very courtyard arguing for English liberal ideas of independence, liberty, and self-government that would one day be used against his masters. In fact, India and its history were tied into the very fabric of Cambridge, from the many leaders who graduated from the university to rule the empire to the many scholars and intellectuals who had studied here and wrote the laws and treatises upon which the empire was based.

Down a narrow alley, I walked toward my college. Clare Hall had more-modern glass buildings, private quarters, right beside a long field. Across the street was the main library.

I went to my room, small by Cambridge standards, but large compared to my Parisian experience. There was a washbasin, a desk, a window, and a door that opened onto bushes and fields. I settled in, took out my few books, the two photos of my parents when they were younger, and my clothes for the coming winter.

By the stroke of a few pens, I had made it to the heart of this foggy island, in my own room without a view, on the banks of the River Cam, in the medieval town of Cambridge, England.

. . .

My dissertation advisor was a man named Stefan Halper, a giant of an American, over six feet tall and three hundred pounds. The first time I saw him, I felt like I was encountering an American version of Hagrid from *Harry Potter*, Halper typing with one finger at a time on his computer. He was a moderate Republican who served in four Republican White Houses, those of Richard Nixon, Gerald Ford, Ronald Reagan, and George H. W. Bush. Around Cambridge, Halper was the sort of man feared and respected, and everyone knew of his ties to Washington. He was also esteemed in intelligence and national security circles, and his reputation was the reason why I had wanted him to supervise my thesis.

We met in his office on the second floor of the sleek new Cambridge building.

I mentioned to him that the GOP was threatening again to shut down the government.

"Who are these piece-of-shit Republicans who keep obstructing for no reason?"

I laughed and felt comfortable with him immediately.

Our conversation moved to China and India, which my master's thesis was going to cover.

"The BRICs are a coinage of Goldman Sachs," he said, referring to the popular acronym at the time for "emerging markets"—Brazil, Russia, India, and China. Everyone was talking about the BRICs and I had the overwhelming sense that this term was nonsense. In under five years' time, all four countries would become more authoritarian.

Halper was telling me about Chinese and Russian influence peddling in Cambridge.

"The premier of China has at least one professor on the payroll," he said. "I see that man and I say to him, 'So, how's the politburo of the Communist Party doing?'"

We spoke about China, about America, the new crop of Republicans who were emerging.

"They aren't Republicans," he said. "They're reactionaries. Who is this asshole, Ted Cruz? Where did he come from?"

Every Friday, Halper, along with Sir Richard Dearlove, the former head of British intelligence during 9/11, held a secretive seminar at Pembroke College. It was said that spies, spooks, double agents lived in and around Cambridge. Conspiracy theories abounded. During the Cold War, spies were also known to be sprawled over Cambridge like mice, the most infamous group called the Cambridge Five, who in the 1930s had secretly passed intelligence to the Soviet Union. These days, the spies hid themselves better. (Halper himself would become notorious in conservative circles in 2016 when he was outed as an FBI informant communicating with Donald Trump's campaign.) If I met a Chinese or Russian spy at Cambridge, they know about it, but I do not. The only time I went to one of these "Intelligence Seminars"—which were in fact dry academic talks—I left out of boredom to bike around town and read on my own.

I preferred to do Cambridge my way, taking long walks, reading at different bends in the river, learning more about the past. I had made India my focus. This was my excuse to study its history. My own interest in India was tied to my forming identity. While not viewing myself as a "Pakistani," I was beginning to feel a connection to the land of united India, the *idea* of India, of Hindustan, as the Persians called it, the subcontinent where Muslims and Hindus and Sikhs and Jains and Christians and Jews lived outside the strictly defined categories of their religion—and *only* their religion, as if caste and class and language and ethnicity did not crisscross all the people from India, who were perhaps the most diverse people in the world, in a million different ways.

I met two Indian students in my college. One was named Kumarjit, a lawyer from Calcutta, a man barely over five feet tall who could consume many shots—he called them "pegs"—of whiskey. (*What the hell is a "peg"?* I wondered. It was about a shot and a half.) The other was Krishna, who was also reading for a master's in international law, having come from one of the most notable legal families in all of India. The three of us would sit together and discuss India.

"Enough of high politics," Kumarjit said. He had a sweet voice and felt like a brother after hanging out only once. "Instead, discuss politics and get high." He raised his glass.

"Tell me something about India," I asked him. "How can Hindu nationalism take over the whole country, with these Narenda Modi types targeting Muslims?" It was sad but true, that at the very time

I wanted to feel closer to the history of India, there was rising in that country a group of right-wingers with an ideology called Hindutva, who believed that India must be a Hindu nation. Muslims and other minorities were but visitors to this land, and Muslims in particular were *invaders*.

"Omer, listen," Kumarjit said, nursing his whiskey. "Don't take this the wrong way, you are my friend, but if I can just give you one piece of advice. You are too Americanized. You have to understand India from within, you know. Don't make the mistake of Westerners who project their own ideology over India. There's too many people there with too many hopes."

"What about Gujarat?" I asked. I was referring to the anti-Muslim riots instigated in the state that Modi was once governor of, and of his own role in the atrocities.

Kumarjit said, "Look, I'm not saying Modi is perfect or that he doesn't have flaws. Fine, the nationalism I can do without. But India is a different country now and the same family has been in charge. Young Indians, they aren't like these Gandhis and their corrupt ways. They are into business, they are entrepreneurs, they want to move ahead. What makes India unique is that it can hold a billion different people together without crumbling.

"Plus, even the Muslims want change!" he continued. "They don't want corruption. I'm not in favor of any sort of religious nationalism or communalism. But India is extremely complicated. It has not been served well by corrupt leaders for decades. The British, you know, the strongman-dictator, it started with them. They called him the *viceroy*."

Brown Boy

My conversations led me to read more about the British Empire. In a very real way, that empire had made me. Britain had conquered, divided, and ruled India for nearly two centuries. Brown people were *still* divided and conquered. India had been plundered for the benefit of the colonizers. Life expectancy in India in 1931 was twenty-seven, according to one estimate. My grandmother was born that year. Colonial India had been her world. Dadiye's parents and their parents, back into the nineteenth century, had only known the British as rulers—and the famines, illnesses, disease, and uncountable deaths that resulted.

I wondered, as I walked the streets of Cambridge, if history was not a process that was continually unfolding, seeming to move forward at times, but always at risk of being thrown backward, always at risk of spinning out of control. There were so many clichés about history: that it rhymed, repeated itself as a farce. I was starting to think of history as the link between generations, a story passed down between cultures and eras. And colonialism was a rupture in that story, a break in the links between fathers and sons, mothers and daughters, whole families broken down and broken up by violence.

At the end of the day, I was only in England because of a longer story that preceded me, a story of colonial terror and violence and migration. And once upon a time, England had indeed been in my own house, in the houses of my forefathers, and had ruled over them with brute force in the name of God and king. Perhaps my being in England now, along with millions of other Brown and Black people, was connected to England being in our homes all those forgotten years ago.

...

Mornings in Cambridge were sacred, a dark blue canvas with the old colleges like silhouettes. Mist hung over the walkways, and I had the sense that great tumults were about to take place in our world.

For the first time in my life, I found myself with the one thing I never had: free time. I had time to waste, time to just think, to relax, to bike, to read, to go punting, to go walking, to go dining, to simply reflect. I moved in different social circles, drinking with the Britishers, hanging with postgraduate students in Pembroke and Darwin College, seeking out discussion wherever I went.

My problem was my liver. I could not keep up with the drinking anymore, and in Cambridge drinking was practically a ritual every night—predinner, during dinner, and afterward. On some evenings, I skipped out of the alcoholic fests and smoked a joint and read.

Carl Sagan, the planetary orbits, the soulful vocals of the Weeknd. I felt a kind of existential awareness in those moments, wanting to laugh at the follies of the world, the self-seriousness of many around me, and my own hypocrisies. While high, I could recall old memories, the way a friend spoke, the smell of an ex-girlfriend, the books I forgot to read, old scenes from old dreams, the tastes and sights and impressions from a time that had vanished. I even laughed at the family that had raised me, the family who seemed more distant to me now than before. (In a bid for moderation, I kept my habit under control. What Fitzgerald had said about liquor applied to marijuana as well: *First you smoke the joint, then the joint smokes a joint, then the joint smokes you.*)

At dawn, it was onto my bicycle, riding through the thousand-year history around me, riding through dark streets and stone walls, rolling past dim lanterns and iron gates, rolling through space-time.

20.

Rivers of Blood

That winter, I took the train to London to take the law school admissions test—for the third time, having messed up the first two. On this icy afternoon, I stepped out into the bustle of King's Cross Station—arching, loud, chaotic, tourists lining up around different platforms. The sounds of slang and street banter floated to me like fragments of verse, and I looked upon more than a few Brown crews, dressed well, speaking in their London slang. Were these East End boys? Or were they from outside of London itself? British Pakistanis and Indians with slick fades talking "innit" and "truss," and many with highbrow accents, making the Queen's English their own.

It was raining that evening as I walked through the streets toward the room I had rented. The London of my imagination had been the city of Dickens: of soot and smoky streets, of lamps and merchant quarters, old bookshops, narrow streets, ashen-faced workers, Fleet Street clubs. The London I encountered was different: a metropolis and city of global capital.

"You good, mate?" said the brother who sold me chai. "Sir, right this way," said the Indian brother who welcomed me to his restaurant. Indian and Pakistani foods were practically the national dishes of England now, and the naan and boti was almost as good as Amma's cooking. Almost.

All night, the rain beat against the windows. I couldn't sleep, thinking how terrible I was at logic games. I thought of another darker-skinned man who had come to London, to become a lawyer, a barrister. I knew his story, had heard his saintlike name repeated in my home. Muhammad Ali Jinnah had been a young man when he had arrived in London; he would read law at Lincoln's Inn and go on to become the founder of Pakistan. I thought of what my father had said when I told him I was going to London. "That's where Jinnah went." Jinnah was always impeccably dressed, a man of English letters who knew Shakespeare by heart, a barrister whose suits were tailored on Savile Row. And he was a good enough Muslim to enjoy his whiskey neat and his ham sandwich at lunch. Indeed, the three major independence leaders—Jinnah, Nehru, and Gandhi—were all lawyers trained in London.

At daylight I went for a walk outside. The LSAT was at noon and I was nervous. The test was held at Ironmongers' Hall, an old building and part of one of the original livery companies that operated under a Royal Charter. I sat for the four-plus-hour exam, and then emerged into a different, darker city. It had been snowing, the air was colder, ice on the sidewalk. I walked onward, reviewing the exam in my head. If I got the score I needed I'd be a competitive applicant at all the top law schools.

I passed a covered bus stop, trying to find Barbican Station, but was so lost in my thoughts I didn't see the grenade falling from above. A ball of ice came flying, landing right at my feet, shattering on the sidewalk. I stopped, turned—and ducked, another ball of ice nearly hitting my head, smashing against the wall of the building next to me.

Quickly, I ran behind a bus booth. A moment of panic, uncertain of what was going on.

Beyond the street was an apartment building where a group of white boys—scrawny, baseball caps, loose clothes—stood. Five or six of them. I thought they were just fooling around until more sharp pieces of ice landed and broke into splinters on the telephone booth in front of me. I could hardly believe what I was witnessing; but this was no time to think. It was time to act.

I stood my ground and faced them. A white fist threw another ice ball right at me—it rose and fell in slow motion, and shattered right at my feet.

A Black woman ran past, covering her head with her purse.

Run or hide.

Another piece of ice flew toward me. Damn these white boys! I wanted to confront them, their scrawny bodies—their arrogant smirks. But I knew if anything bad happened it could lead to me being deported from England. I could see the news now. "Cambridge Student Assaults Three City of London Pupils." Or rather: "Illegal Pakistani Man Attacks Schoolboys." Damn them!

I did not wish to run this time. I wanted to preserve my dignity in the face of intimidation. I was not a kid anymore. But more ice pieces flew toward me. In a split second, I covered my head with my backpack and ran as fast as I could, the ice falling at my heels, one piece striking my leg, shards shattering behind me as I ran through the streets of London, ran with anguish beating in my chest, *ran.*

...

The following month, I was surprised to see an invitation in my student mailbox. It turned out that the patron of the Cambridge Trusts, my scholarships, was visiting the university and wanted to meet the various scholars. I had grown tired of similar invitations and various formal events that never quite lived up to the hype, but I felt obligated to attend this one.

It was raining as I biked up to Fitzwilliam Museum. When I arrived, I walked up the stone steps of the museum and into the large gallery. I was wearing the only suit I owned. Inside were about a hundred students, a hush in the air. I filled my plate with appetizers as the murmurs grew louder.

After thirty minutes of standing idly with a plate in my hands, I saw my patron. His Royal Highness Prince Charles of Wales.

He entered with security through a side door and students quickly lined up to shake his hand.

Prince Charles was a few feet from me. He had on a double-breasted suit, hair combed to the side. He was holding a giant tea mug the size of a bowl, the tea bag on the saucer with a spoon still in the mug, and he walked along making chitchat (*gupshup* in Urdu) with other students.

There he was, right before me, moving in slow motion. The heir to the throne, the future king of Great Britain and the Common-wealth, from the House of Mountbatten-Windsor. Weeks earlier, I had learned with some disappointment that the English family who ruled Britain were actually German, and that their actual last name was not Windsor but Saxe-Coburg-Gotha. In fact, the whole

First World War had been something of a family affair, with most of the European monarchs related to each other.

My hands grew sweaty. What might I say to him? My mind was short-circuited by how improbable all this felt. Me, Charles, Cambridge. Me, from a ramshackle neighborhood in Canada, now face-to-face with the descendant of the long-dead empress of India.

I had never met my grandfather, Dadiye's husband. When my grandfather was a boy, there would have been NO INDIANS AND DOGS signs outside British establishments. The forefathers of the prince had ruled over India and Africa at the time, and here I was, about to introduce myself to the next king of England. I looked around this room full of riches, the consequence of history and violence, our clashing inheritances about to meet. I could pause the tape, rewind it to an earlier time: go back two centuries, to London and Cambridge, and a similar night would be taking place in such an opulent room, the assembled gentlemen toasting to the empire on which the sun never set—but I would have been in India, watching the colonizers arrive.

Dadiye had told me that she and her family fled Amritsar in India just before the midnight hour of Partition struck. They had lived peacefully among their Sikh and Hindu neighbors, sharing in Eid and Diwali festivals. She was a teenage girl of fifteen when the gangs and mobs began ransacking her street. One day she returned to her house to see pages of the Qur'an torn and thrown all over the rooms. And soon she, like millions of others, was on a rickety train, traveling under the cover of night to the new country.

Corpses littered the marshes and fields the train passed. The stench of rot and blood and sweat and fear. Only the royals and upper classes were safe in their mansions and chambers, figuring out the fine legal details of the new states, playing their high politics. There was a huge gap between the men in the palaces and chambers, and the families like my grandmother's, leaving what little they had behind, embarking into the darkness.

I wondered, as I waited to speak to the future king, what my grandmother thought as the train rode through the black night.

Prince Charles looked at me. His face was wrinkled and his pocket square fresh.

"And where are you from?" Prince Charles asked.

I thought of saying British India. I was a child of his family's colonies.

"Canada," I answered.

He smiled knowingly, as if we might see each other again. I looked at him and he at me, men of two completely different backgrounds, who were tied together through the accidents and crimes of history. I let the other arms reach past me to touch him as I fell back into the crowd, drifted outside to the misty English rain, wondering as I left whether the longer arc of history did not eventually come around full circle.

• • •

Later that spring, I was in my room getting ready for my first May Ball, the lavish Cambridge affair that happened at the end of the academic year. In the mirror, I struggled to tie a bow tie for the first time. The horns of a rap song blared out over my room, and it all felt grandiose—except I struggled for three hours trying to tie the bow tie. While glancing at myself, I realized that I was enjoying life in that moment in a way I might never enjoy it again. I could foresee empty days in the future, alone, looking for a job, days where I would reminisce about these very moments that I was now living. As I pulled my black jacket over the starchy white shirt, I was nostalgic for a present that was not yet over.

Who did I feel like, in my black tie? Like a diplomat and spy—a contradiction, yes, but I was used to contradictions by now, and I was headed to the grandest party of my life. My imagination expanded to match the wondrous night.

The Cambridge spring was warm. I strolled happily through the streets, up toward Pembroke College, where various friends were assembled, women in dresses and men in tuxedos, the theme of *The Tempest* around us, people in fancy attire coming and going like moths among the whisperings and the stars.

A friend handed me a little rock the size of a tiny diamond: MDMA, known in my neck of the woods as Molly. I considered it for a moment and then thought, *What the hell*, and swallowed it down. A few seconds later, I felt a burst of euphoria between my temples, an explosive love for all creatures, a boundless compassion for myself and every human on this earth; a love that had been within me this whole time was radiating outward like fireworks.

The courtyard was filled with tents, different parties, a silent disco, wine and cheese over there, various old dons in the corner looking tight-lipped. We danced to the sounds of hip-hop mixed with funk. It was a gorgeous night, the feeling in the air luminous as my lips hummed to the music I could sense in my nerves. It was all ecstasy: the lights and elegant people and music and Cambridge and the dreams of youth ending and beginning within the boundless evening.

A few hours went by. It was past midnight, the sky still lit up with fireworks and song. I looked around and my friends were all dispersed; some eating, some dancing, some sitting and smoking and talking, women with heels in their hands.

There was a straight pathway ahead of me with some bushes, and who did I see but the great English spy himself.

Yes, *that man.*

Bald, bespectacled, paunchy, tuxedoed, a veritable Trojan horse in trousers. It was Sir Richard Dearlove, the former head of MI6—British intelligence.

Sir Dearlove was approaching me. His cheeks were reddish, the old spook having had a few drinks himself. Those watchful eyes were relaxed. I was in such a state of elevation, so full of love for all beings, that I could have reached out and hugged Sir Dearlove.

One cannot overstate how powerful this man was. The world of my adolescence, of my young adulthood, had been shaped as much by Sir Dearlove as by any other man, save for the director of the CIA. All the security protocols; the nightly battles against a secretive enemy; the wiretappings and confidential informants and infiltrators and black sites and dark prisons. Sir Dearlove had a hand in them all. He had led his country through this creation of a new world order, where secret wars were fought at home and abroad to root out an elusive enemy who might be me, or you, or our neighbors.

Sir Dearlove was in front of me now.

"Fine night isn't it?" he said.

I smiled and said, "Indeed, it is."

I thought of saying something more—something political, something disruptive, declaring that we had created more terrorists than we had killed, asking Dearlove whether he knew that violence always turned back on its perpetrators, asking him whether he realized that a generation was coming up who knew only fear and surveillance.

"Sir . . ." I began hesitatingly.

He turned to me. Those eyes narrowed as they must have during his interrogations.

"Yes?" he said.

By the norms of the English upper class, I could not interrupt a pleasantry with a serious intellectual matter. I was ready to transgress the codes of civility among the Cambridge elite, but I stopped myself.

"Have a good night."

Sir Dearlove smiled. We exchanged head nods like we were a pair of hustlers—and the old don walked past me, down the courtyard, into the shadows, taking with him all the secrets only he knew.

. . .

The year at Cambridge ended too quickly. There was no final hurrah but a summerlong race to complete my dissertation. I wanted to go home, study for my law exam again, and apply to law schools in America. I was in a great hurry, much like a sprinter halfway through the race who cannot stop or even pause to look behind him. A legal education would indoctrinate me in the rules of power, and

I wanted to put my education in service of people like me: from the margins, the marginalized, the minorities, the class traitors, the outcasts, the outsiders. After thirteen months at Cambridge, I had been polished and patronized. Now I was prepared.

Every facet of my life had changed. I had learned something about myself and the history that made me. Things happened in rapid succession: the doors that opened led to more flights and travels to distant places, meeting people who were at once like my brothers but also strangers. I traveled to Cyprus, to Hungary, to Jordan, to Iraq—all while a graduate student. I traveled alone, finding myself along the barbed-wire border of Nicosia, the last remaining divided capital in Europe; or in Barcelona with Gaudí's masterpiece before my eyes, admiring the Sagrada Família in silence; or three thousand miles east, in Iraqi Kurdistan during the sweltering heat of Ramadan in July 2013, riding in a jeep through the desert at sunset, 50 Cent playing on the stereo, my Kurdish host reminding me that ISIS was just twenty miles away.

Everywhere I went, I met young people just like myself: outsiders looking in, speaking different languages, working toward different dreams, creating for themselves that which did not yet exist. And I saw that what bound me to young people everywhere was not my name or my heritage alone but an impatience with the way things were, an urgency to reimagine the world, to create something better. History was history, but the future could always be rewritten.

Passion for learning still burned within me. I still had that flaming desire that had started all those years ago at the computer in my parents' house. I was committed to making my mark in the world of foreign policy, and my next destination came into radical focus. I ran again, ran freely toward the land where all dreams were possible, a nation founded upon a universal idea, a restless, relentless republic that was arguing with itself for two centuries, a place where anyone could reinvent themselves and be reborn again: the United States of America.

V.
East–West

21.

Father and Son

Home was like a foreign country now. Having been to college and graduate school, I was thrust back into my former world as a changed man. My mother, father, and grandmother were waiting patiently for my return that August.

"Oh my god!" Amma exclaimed when she saw me. "You are back from England!"

I sat at the table. A great commotion stirred. My father showed up in his pajamas and a sweater. He was still working as a parking officer but was planning to retire soon. "Guess he didn't like eating all the potatoes and meatloaf."

"Eat, eat," Dadiye said. "You must gain weight."

My father and I soon got to work building a study in the house. Since leaving for college, I had accumulated hundreds of books and had nowhere to put them. Together, we tore down a room, painted the walls light brown, and built a bookshelf. It was like I was back in those childhood days watching my father work under the hood of the car, me handing him tools. When the room was done, I finally had a place to study with my books surrounding me, each one a special purchase I had made from a used bookstore.

For weeks, I studied hard for the law exam. I wanted to be a lawyer, and when I was back in this old house, I recalled the times I was a boy hungering for knowledge and impact. Now it was time to deliver. Only Dadiye was in the house, watching Oprah on low volume, as I sat in the next room, neck down, practicing logic games and puzzles for hours.

"Get scholarship," she whispered. "I have seen a dream where you were successful in your exam. I prayed to Allah that this happens."

Dreams were called *khwabs*. My grandmother was always having these dreams; sometimes they portended a coming tragedy, other times they were visions of great happiness. Normally, I wouldn't take these dreams seriously, except for the fact that my grandmother was eighty years old and had seen everything from the rise of Hitler to the election of JFK to the moon landing to Obama's reelection. Her dreams meant something to me, were part of our tradition of elders passing on prophecies to youngsters. She still asked me questions about what she saw on CNN, and we still drank chai in the afternoons between her prayer and my study break, but now I was a little older.

After one terrible dream, Dadiye donated and whispered a prayer over my head.

"May you always stay protected from the Evil Eye," she said.

• • •

Later that fall, my father knocked on the door while I was studying. He did not look at me.

"Are you busy?" he asked.

I was putting in twelve-hour days of studying again, trying to fulfill the promise I had made to myself in that last year of high school of going to a top law school.

A pause. I looked up, saw him, his youthful eyes, but the exhaustion was all over his face.

"No, no I'm not," I said. Something had told me to stop and listen, not brush this attempt at communication aside.

He shook his head. "Never mind. I don't want to bother you. We can talk some other time."

My father's hair was now gray with white streaks, and on weekends, I'd see him in the garage, working with wood, building little shelves and replacing closets. Our relationship had changed since I returned from England; he deferred to me at times, even asked for my advice. In the room now, he was strangely quiet.

Language fails precisely when it is needed most and the words do not come because the emotions do not permit them.

"You focus on your law exam," he said, and left the room.

A few weeks later, I was waiting outside for a ride home from the library. It was November, a chilly evening and the sun was setting behind the brick-and-glass YMCA. I saw my breath and felt tension in my chest: What if I failed this exam? What if I could not go to law school? What if I somehow ended this educational journey right here? What if everything went wrong? What if, what if, what if . . . But the clouds looked like glaciers in the sky and I had not failed yet. Every time I grew too anxious, I would take a deep breath and remind myself, "Your story is over only when you decide it's over," and other little pep talks to keep from getting down.

Dada picked me up. I got in the warm car. It was one of his

last days before retirement and the parking authority was sad to see him go after fifty years of service.

We were driving down clear roads, Urdu radio playing, a woman's voice reporting news from across the world, followed by ads for Pakistani grocers and Indian insurance brokers.

Only then did my father speak.

"I have cancer," he said.

It was like a shot to the neck, the last syllable dropping in deadened silence. I gulped, didn't say a word.

"I haven't told anyone, not even your mother. I don't want the family to stress. Keep it to yourself."

Cancer. Even the word sounded like a final declaration, like a cruel verdict imposed from above, one that collapsed all of one's life into the end zone. But how could this be? the boy in me wondered. Dada had been the strongest man I knew, the one who fixed something when it was broken, a man who took nothing from no one, Miami Aziz, who had made a living in the winters doing jobs others didn't want to do, who enrolled me at the YMCA when I was a toddler because he said South Asians had terrible health outcomes. Two years before this, my father's sister had died suddenly in her sleep. And just a few years before that, my father seemed to be in his prime, going on a walk every day, watching his salt. Time was passing in a new way, speeding up and slowing down simultaneously.

My father was quiet. I could tell he was straining to speak, feeling his own shame at the revelation, as though being diagnosed with cancer was the universe making a moral judgment.

"Doctor found a lump in my neck, cancer of the blood. He

said it was nothing, but I told him, 'Get the bloody test done' after he told me not to worry."

He put the indicator on, took a left turn.

I felt utterly unprepared. We didn't know how long he had or when his treatments would begin. When I was little, my father used to say, "I get sick and I go into work, but when you guys are sick, that's when I take a day off." It felt unfair, but I knew not to say so aloud, for the word *unfair* was not in the immigrant vocabulary. Dada said that life was not equal and complaining got you nowhere. But still, the idea of my father as a mortal man, as someone fighting an inner sickness he could not control, who was having trouble even getting his sentences out, made me realize I had grown up, myself.

"Don't tell your brothers for now," he said as we pulled into the driveway. Oz was finishing up his exams at college and Ali was applying himself. In the moment when my father had the most reason to be selfish, he was worried that news about his health would negatively affect his children's education.

We pulled into the driveway. Neither of us said a word, just sat there. I felt guilty for worrying about the law school exam when there were so many more important things to worry about: health, family, love, our parents, the limited time we had with each other. I tried not to look at my father, at the thinning gray hair, the softness of his eyes, the face that once had filled me with such fear—and I saw the phases of his life flash before me: the student he was in Pakistan, when everyone called him "the human calculator" and said he would become a medical doctor in the West one day; the filing of immigration papers; enrolling in community college and encountering the wider world for the first time; living through the roaring 1970s with long hair and tight jeans; his own dad's early death; the responsibilities suddenly placed on his shoulders to care for the whole family, to bring his mother to Canada, to provide for his wife and children. I don't think he ever fully recovered from the shocks he experienced in life, or else wore them as proud trials he had overcome. And his anger? That must have been the consequence of frustrated hopes. It was the private knowledge he carried throughout his aging years that he could have been so many other things in life if only his circumstances had permitted. The weight of this knowledge must have worn on him.

I thought of what to say. I thought that there was so much more on the line now than my own career. I thought that my mission of academic study had taken on a new significance. I thought that I could not and would not fail. I thought that we would endure this as well and keep another tragedy at bay.

Dada was the one to finally speak. He did not mention the six-letter word or the prognosis.

Instead, he simply asked, "You need me to drop you to the library tomorrow?"

• • •

The diagnosis had come when I was still an undergrad. Dada had kept it a secret for a few years. Eventually, he told my mother and grandmother when he began chemotherapy, though the word was not uttered in our home. This family had always worked in silences, and these silences would continue—this was our habit, as though the realities of fate had to be faced stoically, without public displays of emotions.

Amma said, "We must forgive and help because this is a test from Allah."

I drove him to his next appointment, taking my studying materials with me while he went into the doctor's office. It was an unseasonably warm fall day, the comings and goings of the street seeming especially mundane, people living their lives without the chest-tightening feeling that their time was finite.

A few minutes into the drive, I found that I was truly enjoying myself. Dada spoke freely about his usual topics: commenting on politics, on Pakistan, on hockey and basketball, and all the "crooks and politicians stealing from the workingman." Maybe it was this constant feuding with the world that had kept him going, the same quarrelsome energy that kept my grandmother going, with all those beefs with *dushman* and enemies only they knew about.

He called himself Miami at the clinic. He lay back as the nurses talked with him. I waited outside and did a practice exam. When I was allowed to see my father, a charming nurse said, "Your father was joking the whole time. He said he wanted medical marijuana." Miami was in good form and I saw a lesson in that, too: when the world mocked you, you mocked the world right back.

Dada had never been close to anyone, but I realized how my father and I were not that different. He was the brash immigrant who was fearless in sharing his opinions, even if he valued safety above all else. I was the son of immigrants born on this soil who was willing to look beyond the safety nets and take risks in pursuit of my dreams. We were mirrors of each other in certain ways, both of us with big imaginations that could be not curtailed by those around us.

Nazar was always evoked during talks about health or success. *Nazar* was the Evil Eye, the forbidding fate, the fear that conceit cometh before the fall. *Nazar* was the ever-present truth that life could punish us if we got full of ourselves. And worse than *Nazar* was the fear of being pitied.

"Some of our people are cunning," Dada used to say before listing off the hundreds of examples of one Brown person screwing over another. He said this selfishness was why Pakistan and India were so corrupt, because in those countries the weak were constantly being exploited by the strong, and the rich were bleeding their country for all its wealth.

I drove my father home. He was tired and didn't wish to speak. For some months, we did not mention his cancer, not unless he brought it up with an update like "Now they are giving the poison they give to bloody rats! This is modern medicine! Rat poison!" And these conversations ended with the same admonishment that I not let news of his illness affect my studies.

Over these same months, I was terrified of the prospect that I would strike out at all the top law schools and would say goodbye to my dreams. I kept my fears hidden. In reality, I was scared and knew that my luck could change at any moment. I could not imagine a world without my father, and yet I knew that day would come. One day I would have to step up and care for my family. So much more was on the line, but I had to push aside my doubts, act "as if" I were confident. I had learned that pretending to act self-assured was a defense against the dark insecurities in my heart.

On the day of the exam, I got to the study hall early. I had prepared like I was an Olympic athlete, running drills from seven in the morning to nine at night. Two hours into the test, someone pulled the fire alarm. Students panicked, months of hard work potentially going to waste. I did my best to stay in Zen-focus, kept my breathing in check, and finished the exam. Living with a loud family where the verbal alarms went off at all hours had finally come in handy.

Afterward, all I had was prayer and hope. I applied to Harvard and Yale. I had to withdraw my application from Stanford Law because they wanted to know what had happened in Paris and required a form from my college dean, who I did not know personally. There were many boxes to check to even be eligible at these elite schools—this was how the top 1 percent guarded the gates of meritocracy. Harvard Law School eventually put me on their wait list. My hopes were riding on the best law school in the world, and really the only law school I wanted to attend.

Then I was wait-listed at Yale, too.

I sent the dean a letter explaining why I only wanted to attend Yale Law. Was it crazy to pin all my hopes on Yale? A little bit. But I reasoned that I should give myself a shot at the top, especially at a place where misfits and outcasts were known to be accepted. I also wanted to destroy the Brown kid syndrome of settling for much less out of fear and scarcity. It was in my immigrant family's blood to accept, without complaint, whatever was handed to us—and I hoped to eviscerate that inborn shame, the inner self-limitations that wondered, *What will people say?* and *Am I good enough?* and *Should I give up now?*

There was also the small matter of finances. The Ivy League came with a $100,000-a-year price tag on the surface, but because of need-blind admissions and generous financial aid packages, Yale Law School would cost less than almost any law school in Canada or America.

In August, just weeks before classes were to begin, a 203 area code lit up my phone. I was in downtown Toronto, in a suit, when I nervously heard the voice of the dean of admissions at Yale Law School.

"Congratulations," he began . . . and the rest was a blur.

I had been admitted to Yale Law School. Moreover, I received a financial aid package that covered the entire cost of attendance, roughly a fifty-fifty split between scholarships and university loans.

Breathless and dizzy, I walked those Toronto streets like I was just drafted into the NBA. The August sunshine beamed on my face. I sauntered through the Financial District, smiling to myself amid the rushing faces and briefcases, treasuring this moment of arrival. I thought back to the long nights of writing vocabulary lists with a shaky pencil, of feeling estranged from my community, of being isolated from family and friends.

America had called for me, and I was about to enter the chaos of the republic at a crucial moment in history. I wanted to savor the acceptance a little longer, for I knew that in the past I had denied myself any feelings of satisfaction. But there was simply no time to bask in romantic ideas about arrival. I had to get my papers in order. I knew those border guards would ask for them.

22.

Amerika

By the time I got to New Haven, I had come to accept the folk-lore of America as the embodiment of greatness. America was where inventions changed the world. America was the land of poets and churchgoers, of Black intellectuals and Latino artists: a melting pot where everyone, by its written Constitution, was equal. America was the oldest democracy in the world and the first large republic since Rome to exist for more than a handful of years. America was the only country based on an idea: that all people are created equal. America was a nation with the soul of a church. Though I had read about the civil rights movement, had studied Martin and Malcolm, I felt that there was something essential America got right: its moral aspirations to be good. These myths were about to be challenged.

I rented a first-floor apartment on the corner of Elm Street, three blocks from the university. It was explained to me that I was living at the border between New Haven and Yale Haven—travel just one block farther, as I did on my first day, and you would see broken houses, kids on bikes, and not a white face in sight.

The first thing I noticed about New Haven as I walked to Yale Law School was how segregated the city appeared. I walked down

Elm Street, past the trees, the liquor store, a smattering of police cars and homeless men around me. There were a handful of young Black boys hanging around, shooting the shit and just chilling on a school day. The fact that Yale was just a few blocks away struck me as a cruel mockery. This was not the *banlieue* or Scartown, but an underclass condemned in perpetuity. And the border between the Black part of the city and the university was clear and could have been drawn with a red line down the road.

I walked on and soon arrived at the law school, on the opposite end of the class spectrum, with Oxbridge-style buildings and grassy courtyards and monuments to great men of the past. I saw sweater-vests and cardigans and suits, fresh-faced students walking like the world was theirs to conquer. It was a world full of possibilities, the law school walls plastered with posters advertising leaders coming to our classrooms to speak: the treasury secretary, a Supreme Court justice, or Hillary Clinton. The students here were some of the smartest in the world. Yet I felt the tension split my mind as I started classes, of being part of an exclusive club, but standing on the edges. Progressivism was the dominant ideology at the law school, yet we were part of an elite whose sole purpose, it seemed, was to reproduce itself and keep ordinary people out.

The dean of the law school addressed us during Orientation Week.

"You're off the treadmill now." The dean said we should study the goals associated with the law: justice, fairness, accountability. We should define success for ourselves and pursue our own experience of law school. In America, the dean said, quoting Thomas Paine, the law was king.

I stopped taking notes. For my whole education, I had been consumed by grades, scores, exams, competitions, scholarships, put through the meritocracy tunnel, getting badges that would show the world that I was good enough. Now I could at last relax a little, throw overboard these artificial metrics of knowledge.

Another professor addressed us. He had a bald head and goatee. "If you are not white, Yale was built to exclude you," he said. "For the majority of Yale's history, all of you who are not white would not be welcome here." The professor's clarity was refreshing. Yet I did not feel like such an impostor anymore. I felt like I had the right to be here. I had worked hard, had come from a working family, and therefore could be confident. Of course, everyone in the elite believed some version of the success-as-evidence-of-virtue story. This system of privilege, I would soon learn, was about inculcating certain assumptions about how the world worked.

Well, now that you're here, are you going to just settle into the comfortable patterns of achievement—clerkship, making partner at a law firm—or pursue your own curiosities?

I decided right there that I would take the dean at his literal word. I would work to apply what I was learning in the world, to gather interesting people in my apartment and discuss ideas with them, to read American history and literature and write every moment I could. I would study America as my subject, both its constitution and its foreign policy. Law, after all, was not merely a series of cases and judicial opinions. It was the record of a long-running story, a nation arguing with itself, a language that revealed the contours of every structure in economics and politics. And I would seek to make my mark on foreign policy. Yale Law School was going to be as close to a pure creative and intellectual experience as possible: three years of freedom to chase after questions that excited me, to ask questions of the powerful, to live the intellectual life, return to first principles, relearn everything from scratch, not just the case-books of American law but the assumptions behind those laws. I was one out of many, and I was ready for the infernal heat of the American furnace.

I settled into my apartment with the small wooden table and chair, wooden floors, stacks of books around me. *Lux et Veritas*, light and truth, was Yale's motto—and now my own.

· · ·

Entering Yale Law School is like walking into a gorgeous mansion with hundreds of rooms. I was initially disoriented and unsure where to go. Each door led to its own path and I did not know where to take a right or a left. All doors were available, but some were guarded by powerful men and women who required codes to let me through. Beyond these doors were still others, depending on how close to the center of power they were. Particular signals and cues were needed to pass into these special zones. If you come from a nonprofessional background, you question whether you were admitted to this mansion by accident. There are many guests, each one of them impeccably dressed. What the newcomer often does not see are all the hidden networks between these friends and colleagues that allowed them to get there in the first place and will propel them forward, the subtle hierarchy that makes this person worth talking to and gets that person ignored.

And then I would look out at crumbling New Haven from

the windows of the law library, and I would see the gates, visible and invisible, between the ivory tower and the street. My people, I always felt, were on the other side of those gates. What I understood by now was that I was entering the elite and would need to act accordingly. That meant knowing the permissible boundaries of thought, what to say, what not to say, how to carry oneself in powerful circles of conversation. I had been to college, to graduate school, had lived in Paris, but I stuck out among the elite of Yale Law, where the top students went to be trained to one day run the United States government. Senior Obama administration officials had decamped for Yale, and the law school was becoming an ideas hub for policy like Harvard during the Kennedy years. Students at Yale openly joked about the "revolving door between Washington and Wall Street," and they meant 127 Wall Street, the address of Yale Law School. Power was in the air here.

But it was not race that made me feel out of place at Yale as much as class. Should I talk to them straight-up, share my ideas, ask questions? Should I imitate their reserved manners, hiding my true views, lest I upset the person I was talking to? Should I spout every generic sentiment that good liberals knew by heart and would put me politely in the middle—and therefore nowhere? Or would I truly try to be myself: curious, observant, opinionated, willing to provoke?

The imposter in me said, *Be like everyone around you.*

I made friends sparingly, intimidated not by their knowledge but their withering judgments. Most of the students were very liberal and very rich, and there was apparently no paradox in being in the most exclusive club in the world while homeless men languished just blocks from the law school buildings. I was part of the elite club now, so I was irritated with myself as well, arguing my way through the guilt. This was America, and I had come to understand that privilege and poverty lived side by side, separate but equal.

Many students were already chummy with professors, working as research assistants or meeting for drinks after class. There were silos everyone lived in: Republicans whispering only to Republicans, Democrats talking to Democrats. Students on the left went out of their way to shame and blame each other if someone was insufficiently progressive or wanted to work at a big firm or didn't agree that such-and-such speaker should have been *banned* from giving a lecture at Yale. Pile-ons would occur with students one-upping each other, condemning the blasphemous talk. Meanwhile, because conservatives were outnumbered, they gathered underground and did not openly share their opinions with anyone outside a trusted circle. There was a sly and underhanded approach to conversations that at times were little more than elaborate performances.

The Scartown boy in me said, *Fuck these social rules.*

I told myself that these unwritten rules didn't matter, but I knew better. I was caught between dogmas. Liberals wanted to minister to me as though I was a victim. Conservatives wanted to educate me like I was a savage. With liberals, the attitude translated to "Let *us* help *you*," which meant "Helping you is good for me." With conservatives, it was the opposite: "Let us civilize you," with the subtext being "At least you're one of the good ones." The two dogmas squared off, and you were expected to slide into a premade box. I resisted this every day. I was a complex human being and wanted to be treated only as an equal.

Desperate not to slip into invisibility, into *yessir*-ing them all, I made sure to be vocal about my views. I only began to lose my feeling of alienation when I invited friends to my apartment, where we could let loose and talk freely.

Sometimes, my friend Zain would come over—Zain being a Brown kid from the Toronto suburbs who was often mistaken for me even though we looked nothing alike. We usually talked about how we were outliers in our families and how normal isolation felt to us. One night, Zain told me that he didn't believe in rationality, that there was an irrational madness beneath our laws, within our minds. I had to sit with that for a moment, and other friends challenged him on it. I befriended a Lebanese American student, Khalil, who had served in Afghanistan for the United States Army, and who told me his experience of being an American soldier while the world was blaming Muslims for terrorism. Another student named Sameer questioned the American assumptions about democracy that others took for granted. A woman named Lina shared book recommendations with me and commentary about different intellectuals. Jason, a white liberal from Georgia, told me the history of the South and how the South felt that the Civil War had never ended.

Through these nightlong conversations, I began to lose some of my frustration and began enjoying my time at law school. I sought out different arguments, made friends with conservatives and veterans and Latinos and Black people and white people from the working class, keeping open to different perspectives. I had come from nowhere, belonged to no one, and this very invisibility allowed me to be on friendly terms with everyone, willing to learn from and challenge all of them.

I had finally found my footing, and was soon speaking, writing, and living with an energy I thought I never had.

. . .

Later in my first year, I was rushing down Chapel Street, past the bookstores and cafés, to meet with a young law professor named Jake Sullivan. I had accepted that if I wanted to do well in this world, I had to be fearless in reaching out to professors and students, introducing myself, and asking if they wanted to get a coffee. Learning how to approach someone cold—even over email—was a skill I had to learn the hard way, simply by doing it. What amazed me was how often people said yes. I chalked this up to the democratic spirit of Americans, who were inclined to look favorably upon a young person who broke conventions and was hungry to learn.

The week before, I had sent Jake a note telling him of my interest in Syria and US foreign policy. He agreed to meet without hesitation. Jake was a unique figure at the law school: he had been Hillary Clinton's top policy advisor, had run the Policy Planning Staff at the State Department, and would in a few years serve as national security advisor to President Joe Biden. He was teaching at Yale only temporarily. I was nervous before our first encounter.

I got to Starbucks and sat at a table near the back. I scrolled through my phone, making notes of questions I wanted to ask him. Not career advice, but geopolitical questions—What did he think of Russia? Of Xi Jinping, the Chinese president? And of the leadership in Iran, with whom Jake had negotiated in secret to open nuclear talks? In fact, Jake was flying to Geneva the next morning for final negotiations with the Iranian foreign minister. Unlike others who might have approached Jake, I didn't have an interest in trying to get a White House job, but just wanted to absorb the lessons Jake had learned through hard-won experience. After all, Barack Obama and Hillary Clinton had relied on his counsel, so there was much for me to learn.

I saw a skinny, sandy-haired man in a crisp blue collared shirt approach my table with a smile.

"Sorry I'm late," Jake said, extending his hand. He had a long face, thin hair, and the cool, intelligent eyes of someone accustomed to negotiating with Iranian hard-liners.

Jake ordered a green tea. I had coffee.

"So," he said, looking at me, "what's your story?"

I smiled and told him. My answers were much better rehearsed now than they were even a few years before. Jake nodded along indifferently, but when I told him I went to public schools, it was as though I had struck a familiar note.

"I went to public schools in Minnesota," he said.

Now it was my turn to ask a question.

"What do you think is the greatest geopolitical challenge facing the United States?"

Jake didn't flinch. "Without a question, China." We went back and forth over the reasons why, and talked about the last six years of the Obama administration: Syria, Iran, the Arab Spring, China, Russia, international trade.

When we discussed Syria, I made the case that under the Obama administration more could have been done in Syria. Jake was receptive to the point, even if he pushed back and argued that any other policy—humanitarian intervention for instance—would come with its own trade-offs and costs. We talked about life in general, freely, as if we had known each other from back in the day.

"Do you know what you want to do?" Jake asked.

"I have no idea," I blurted out. "I want to focus on foreign policy," I said. "I don't just want to sit on the sidelines. I want to serve."

Jake nodded. I assumed that someone like Jake had come from the glittering capitals of wealth and had been reared at the top private schools like so many others at Yale. But no, he was from more modest beginnings. Despite our differences in age and color, we both had gone to public schools and come from families where the idea of going to Yale Law would have seemed beyond our reach. Yet here we were.

"A lawyer can do a lot more than work in corporate practice," Jake said. "Every morning in the White House there's the President's Daily Briefing. You have the president, who is a lawyer. The vice president, also a lawyer. The national security advisor, a lawyer. The chief of staff—not a lawyer, but knows the law better than most attorneys. I think the harder question you have to ask yourself is where you want to make a difference."

I stayed silent and let him speak. Jake said, "Focus on doing good work. Don't worry about titles and accolades. Focus on the work. The rest will follow."

This was music to me: the idea that I could forge my own path and not worry about what other people would say. The emphasis on the work itself, on the middle-class ethic of rolling up our sleeves and just getting to it, was one of the core values we would return to over the next three years.

Jake and I talked for a few more minutes. He agreed to supervise my major law school paper and we shook hands and said we would meet again soon.

I walked through New Haven elated. I had been taken seriously. I had communicated without trying to please or win favor. My grounding was ideas—and the desire to put ideas into practice. That nexus of thought and action is where I wanted to be. Perhaps I could put this education to good use for people who came from working- and middle-class families who were caught up in a world defined by those at the top. For so long, I had been on the outside looking in. Now with some privilege of my own, I wanted to do something meaningful for people left behind.

. . .

Over the course of that year and after the presidential race, Jake and I would have conversations about America's role in the world. I took two of his classes and he became a kind of mentor. During conversations in Jake's office and in class, we talked about Vladimir Putin and Ukraine and Afghanistan and North Korea and cybercrime. We debated whether the United States was too quick to punish other countries with economic sanctions. We discussed the merits and demerits of arming Ukrainian rebels. Jake would have students debate each side of the issue, one group representing the US president and secretary of state and the other representing their counterparts. He expected us to argue our opponent's position better than they could, and he had me play Sergei Lavrov, the Russian foreign minister, in a debate on international law in Syria. I made sure to look extra grim that day.

At the law school, and in the quiet of my own mind, I spent my time reflecting on the values of America. If America represented something good abroad, it had to be the principles that were being fought for at home—equality, dignity, opportunity. Foreign policy and domestic policy were inherently entwined, and the great test of America's example was how it treated its most vulnerable, its sick, its wounded, at home.

Jake Sullivan posed a question that haunted me: Did American exceptionalism even exist, and if so, what did it mean?

I kept asking myself some version of this question.

Was America a good country?

Was America evil?

Was America moral, immoral, or amoral?

Was America the land of white supremacy? A bastion of slavery and deprivation for Black people, extermination for the Indigenous, and castration for that other despised minority: the poor?

Was America a nation that pretended to worship God but really worshipped money and celebrity?

Was America a place where all things were possible?

Was America a city upon a hill, or an armed fortress keeping out the undesirables?

Was America a nation written into existence through language or barbarism?

Was America the Statue of Liberty or the statue of Robert E. Lee?

America contained multitudes of hope and darkness. I had

never bought the idea that America was an unparalleled force for evil—a view that was common enough since 9/11. There were human rights violations, Guantánamo Bay, torture, and plenty of other areas to indict the United States government for breaking its own laws and behaving in a criminal manner. There were countless historical examples—especially from the Cold War, of America overthrowing democracies or assisting dictators, from Chile to Iran to Indonesia. But as the world stood, America was indispensable to the functioning of a global system of rules that, without American blood and treasure, could crumble and give us the anarchy of the 1930s.

Slavery was written into the Constitution, even though the word was never used. The Fugitive Slave Clause required the forced return of the enslaved. The Electoral College strengthened slavery by empowering the South. America's Constitution enshrined that Black people were two-fifths chattel. Indeed, the Congress could not even legislate to limit the transatlantic slave trade for twenty years after the Constitution went into effect. *Plessy* and *Dred Scott* were shorthand for an apartheid republic.

A retort would point to the laws and amendments that developed in response to liberate the dispossessed: the Declaration of Independence; the Emancipation Proclamation; the Thirteenth, Fourteenth, and Fifteenth Amendments; the Civil Rights Act of 1964; the Voting Rights Act of 1965; not to mention the bloodiest war in American history.

But it wasn't only slavery. Under the very first immigration law passed by Congress, entry into the United States was limited to "free white persons." Every immigration law thereafter, until

1965, imposed racial quotas so strict that, as Yale Law professor James Whitman has shown, Hitler's Nazis drew inspiration from them. White supremacy was codified into the very founding of the country and demonstrated through the enslavement of Africans and the annihilation of Indigenous peoples. After years of war and terror, the United States was withdrawing, turning inward. America was overdue for a period of reflection and contemplation. Four hundred years overdue.

My friend Zain's comments about not believing in rationality stayed with me when I thought of the United States, Amerika, *Amreeka*. I knew that at any prior point in history, my being in the Republic would have been preposterous. And now, as an on-looker and observer, I saw how America was beginning to critique itself with ferocity. The progressive narrative was fracturing; the conservative consensus had shattered. Perpetual wars abroad and discontent at home had wearied the people. A once proud and boastful nation had lost its faith.

The twilight of the Obama era was approaching—and I stood as witness on the border of this American chaos, wondering whether an irrational madness might not swallow us all.

23.

A Nightmare on Elm Street

My first summer of law school I ended up working at the United Nations in Geneva as a legal clerk. Jake Sullivan had helped me find the contact information of the person running the department and I did the rest: introducing myself, explaining why I wished to spend the summer there. I was to work at the Office of the UN Special Envoy for Syria, which was holding consultations with all the warring parties to the Syrian conflict.

Since college, I had watched the Arab Spring transform into a desolate winter in the Middle East. What had started as a revolution of the young morphed into a counterrevolution of the police state—and nowhere suffered as much as Syria. What began as peaceful protests for reform turned into an uprising for democracy and then a civil war and, finally, a full-blown war on civilians with Bashar al-Assad as the chief villain.

I had my own ideas for solving the conflict—intensifying diplomacy, imposing costs on Assad for his genocidal policies, helping the Syrian opposition and disaffected regime members in forming a unity government. But the consequences of any policy could be dire. Jake's words rang in my ears: "Imagine you're sitting in the Oval Office and the president turns to you and asks for your recommendation. Someone like President Obama is going to ask lots of questions, especially about unintended consequences." Every policy maker operated with imperfect information, faced imperfect choices, in an imperfect environment. That said, the consequences of *inaction* could be just as terrible—if not worse.

In Switzerland, I saw the beautiful peaks of Mont Blanc, the clean streets and inconspicuous banks, the waterfalls where one could take a drink right from the stream. I spent the summer near Lake Geneva, in an opulent, Versailles-like building called the Palais des Nations. It was here that the League of Nations, the predecessor to the UN, had been housed and was doomed to fail after the First World War. The palace was a grand masterpiece of marble and stone, with the flags of every country in the world represented. The UN's second headquarters was built to embody the ambitions of a generation scourged by war. But the contrast between the palace's heights and the brutal reality in Syria seemed like a cruel juxtaposition.

I went into work. I read reports. I made my recommendations. The war in Syria dragged on. On Damascus's streets, the regime's thugs spray-painted *Assad or we burn the country*. Meanwhile, the Syrian opposition was splintering. Bashar al-Assad sent his emissary to Geneva to utter generic talking points, while Assad continued bombing hospitals and using chemical weapons against civilians.

As July turned to August, I spent every day in the office trying to find a creative solution for peace talks. Everyone had gone on vacation by now; the office was empty and I roamed the halls that had been constructed in the aftermath of the First World War. That war, followed by a global pandemic, the roaring twenties, and the depressive thirties, gave way to an even greater war and the rise of fascism.

In the very room where the League of Nations had met, I could see the clouds gathering outside the palace, spasms of lightning in the distance. It was clear by now that no breakthrough would be coming. Assad did not want to negotiate. Russia was not interested in stopping the carnage. And America was more invested in defeating ISIS. Syria would remain a holocaust of mass death. History, if not repeating itself, was rhyming once again.

The United Nations had failed in Syria. "Never Again" happened on our watch, in the cities and towns of that ancient country where hundreds of thousands of civilians died under barrel bombs and gas attacks, millions more became refugees, and the bodies of little children washed up on shores. An entire generation—my generation of Syrians—was to know only starvation, bloodshed, and death. I only wished the UN and US could have done more—but Syria was annihilated, and Bashar al-Assad would win.

I felt guilty for having to leave Geneva, like a typical Westerner who had participated in a diplomatic farce and was now retreating back to safety. This was harsh self-criticism, for the truth was that I could not change the outcome. Maybe no one could have. Still, as I headed back to America, I drew inspiration from the young Syrians risking their lives for democracy. Some privileges I had as a Westerner—the right to think, speak, and vote—I might take for granted. Syrians had perished for those rights. They died for the principles of self-government that one day would stain the history books when the Syrian war was remembered. I thought of what an anonymous Syrian had yelled at an Assad regime sniper during the siege of Homs, an epigram and manifesto for my generation:

The world is not yours alone
There is a place for all of us
You don't have the right to own it all.

• • •

Later that August, the cab whisked me from Union Station in New Haven toward my apartment.

The breeze was warm and fresh, one of those quiet New England nights that I loved. We cruised past the green yard, the stars and stripes of the flag fluttering, Yale feeling like a lofty promise as the new semester began. I would prepare for law firm interviews, but I was fixated on the novel I was reading: *The Great Gatsby*. I found something gorgeous in the sense of infinite loss and eternal illusions that the book captured. For whatever reason, I also felt that something was wrong—or could go wrong that night. It was merely an apprehension, and I dismissed it as frayed nerves.

I got back to my apartment on Elm Street. Everything was where I had left it: the books, the table, the poster of Raphael's *The School of Athens* on one side and a Muhammad Ali poster on the other. It was good to be back in this temporary home. I sat down at my desk and began to review my résumé. It was 11:30 p.m. Every summer, partners from the major firms in New York and Washington descended onto campus to meet the best legal talent in America. They interviewed us about our interests, wined and dined us, and dangled lucrative offers for work. There was an elaborate dance that one had to perform, keeping silent on the most important subject of all. It was my misfortune to be slightly too honest at one of my interviews. When a partner at the prestigious firm of Wachtell, Lipton, Rosen & Katz asked me why I wanted a job there, I laughed and said, "Because I need the money!" He was stone-faced, scratched out some notes, and said, "Thank you." I wasn't given a second interview.

My father's advice was to take whatever offer I got. He was an immigrant, so he valued financial safety first. But me: I wanted to live. I wanted to create. I wanted to engage in public service. I wanted to dream. I wanted to write. And I knew myself enough to realize that I had been trained by the rules of the meritocracy, meaning hard work, sacrifice, and following the rules, so I could look down the line and see a future where I was trying to become a law partner, miserable with my life, and suffering from depression. If I was resistant to the idea of a big corporate firm, it was because I knew I would hustle until I dropped in the next logical phase of the rat race.

Still, I didn't want to go against the herd. I did what was expected of me, even though I secretly despised the whole performance of auditioning for these roles. The lawyer in me was answering all my doubts. So what if you have to represent tobacco companies and oil companies? So what if the climate kills us and there are refugees around the world and inequality is the worst since the Gilded Age? The point of an elite degree is to move up endlessly and keep your options open. As Harold Koh, Yale Law professor and former legal advisor to the State Department, once said in class, "Even if you win the rat race, you're still a goddamned rat!"

I felt satisfied at my ability to rationalize myself into delusion. I had become lost in my thoughts, reading in my room, when suddenly—

Pop. Pop. Pop. Pop.

"Ah, fuck man!" a voice shouted outside.

I jumped out of my chair, flicked the lights off, and crouched down. Gunshots had blasted off right outside my window.

The first thing I did was check my body in the darkness to make sure I wasn't hit, for I had read that when you've been shot the body goes into shock and numbs the pain.

My phone buzzed. The downstairs neighbors, who lived in the basement, said they were hiding with their dog under the bed.

I heard my breath. I saw nothing. I felt the sweat drip from my forehead and hit the wooden floor like a crack of thunder. My apartment had several large windows and was right on the ground floor, so the shooting had happened just feet from me.

Suddenly, there was shuffling outside my door. I peeked out through the blinds. There was a Black boy, roughly eighteen, lying on the steps right outside, blood splattered over his legs. His friend was standing by him trying to get him to calm down.

"Ah, man! I been shot!" said the boy, clutching his leg.

Slowly, I stood up. I kept my back close to the wall, in case more bullets popped off. I could hear that boy's cries. My mind raced. I went to the door. The apartment was still dark. I looked through the peephole and saw his friend pacing.

What was I supposed to do? I knew the code of the streets: it was dangerous to be a witness. You saw nothing, did nothing, and never got involved in other people's business. Whoever had fired their gun might still be around. I might be called on as a witness, now roped into a beef that wasn't mine. I would have told anyone in my position to stay the hell inside. But no one had come to help. No one had bothered to even open their door. The boy with the gunshot wound was right on the porch steps. I thought of what my mother would do. Didn't she say that our faith required us to help those in need? And if I, a Yale law student, couldn't help one of these boys, then I was as useless as the paper my law degree would be written on.

I took a breath and opened the door.

The scene froze before my eyes. Every door on the street was shut and every window closed. The street looked abandoned. Two feet from me was the boy lying on the stairs, trying to turn and see me. His friend eyed me suspiciously. They were both teenagers.

"You all right?" I asked. "You guys need water?"

My voice was shaking. The boy was clutching his legs. There was a hole the size of a dime in his leg and it had made his jeans dark red.

The boy who'd been shot yelled, "Somebody get my phone!"

His friend handed it to him.

Sirens, lots of them, grew louder and louder, heading in our direction. My first thought was *Please don't let this get out of hand.*

The friend, a Black boy with a long T-shirt, stared up at me. "Can I use your bathroom?"

Again, I hesitated. The lawyer in me knew this was a crime scene and I should have just stayed inside. But I couldn't now say no.

He walked right through the apartment and I heard the bathroom door close. The faucet turned on. The toilet flushed. I paced back and forth, checking on the wounded friend, getting him water, and then going back inside.

After a few moments, his friend came out.

"Appreciate you," he said as we went back outside.

Three police officers had arrived and began questioning the boy who'd been shot. The cruisers still had their lights flashing; they bounced off the houses, red and blue hues. Another siren blared, the ambulance coming.

One officer stood by the porch with his feet apart and his hands on his hips.

"You do any drugs tonight?" he asked the boy.

"Just smoked some weed, man!" the wounded boy shouted.

"What happened tonight? You got into an altercation?"

The boy mumbled an answer and then cried out in anger, "Somebody shot me, can't you see?"

The cop asked the friend where the bullets had come from. The friend pointed to the other side of the street, close to Popeyes.

"Did you see who shot you?" the officer asked.

The boy gave a description of a generic Black male.

"Do you know him?"

The boy screamed, "I don't know!"

I stood and watched the entire interaction, unable to move. It was all done matter-of-factly, business as usual for the cops. It was like there was no boy suffering from a bullet wound, just another random shooting on a random New Haven night.

The police didn't ask me anything. I was relieved. It was almost as if I wasn't even standing there, a Brown man between the white cops and the Black teenagers. Their silence made me want to say something, but I stayed quiet.

Two paramedics helped the boy onto a stretcher. The friend grabbed his backpack and disappeared into the ambulance. The cops drove away. I went back inside and shut the door.

It was dark in my apartment—dark and humid. I slumped down on the couch. I saw droplets of blood on my floor.

Violence had brought itself to my doorstep, had nearly terminated my body. The difference between life and death was an angle of a few degrees.

I thought of whether to call my mother and tell her—no, she would panic. I thought of Shilton and the friends from high school who had died before they were old enough to graduate. This could have been that teenager's last night, and he would have died for nothing—another statistic, another number, to be forgotten just as quickly. And I knew that those boys would probably encounter the law again, that it was only a matter of time before they slipped up, and next time they might not be so lucky. The laws—of the state, of the streets—would entangle them soon enough. One could almost guarantee it. America's prisons depended on a steady supply of fresh faces to keep the machine moving. This was the brutality of America, where young people shot and killed each other over candy bars and girls or for simply looking the wrong way. And to think that just minutes prior I was fretting about law firm interviews.

I felt the old, familiar fear in my skin—a fear I could not outrun or escape. I wiped the blood from my floor. The room felt warped, like it was closing in on me, coffinlike. In the middle of the night,

I woke up breathing heavily. I pulled the blinds. The porch was empty, still stained. I sat on the edge of the bed and the night replayed itself: the whip crack of gunshots, the boy bleeding on the stairs, the ghost town of a street. It was the normalcy of it all that struck me as grotesque.

I tried to sleep, to forget about the shooting. Tomorrow would be another long day of pretending to fit in.

. . .

Law school wasn't the same after that. The shooting had shifted something in me and I longed to escape the confines of the classroom. I began to go down to New York every weekend. I felt safer in the city, among the throng of bodies and accents and the great tumult of Manhattan. Each step I took in New York made me roil with electric tension. New York was the woman I loved. New York was the hustle and high drama of unrealized dreams. New York was a golden bookstore, open late at night, my nose pressed against the window, a light shining on the books inside. New York was the immigrant, the striver, the girl starting from the bottom. I felt like an exile in the city of exiles.

I walked through the Village, through the Bowery, the Upper West Side, imagining the writers and intellectuals who had passed by on these streets, imagining the waves of new faces who showed up here, Jews and Italians and Irish, speaking in foreign tongues, feared and loathed by the established citizens. I watched the boys freestyling on the street corner and was reminded of my boyhood in Scartown. I saw the marvelous trees of Central Park and recalled that Nabokov had said that winter trees resembled the nervous systems of giants. When a group of Orthodox Jews passed me, I felt kinship with them, for they were going to the synagogue to recite the Torah the way I had gone to the mosque to recite the Qur'an. "Jewish?" they asked me. I was surprised. "Not today," I answered cheerfully.

In New York, the sounds of free verse were everywhere. The beat of different registers reverberated around me and I heard in them all of America's tempos. The progress that New York symbolized, and Obama embodied, was coming undone. Donald J. Trump, son of New York, was rising in the polls. Everyone back at Yale Law treated him as a clown, and people openly joked about how badly he would lose. (I heard reports from my father that my grandmother would sit up in her seat when Trump would appear on CNN and hurl Urdu and Punjabi insults his way.)

I suspected that Trump had a better shot than most people thought he had: after all, he spoke to white people who were angry, and I had learned never to doubt the power of white rage. Trump's slick blond hairstyle made him a cartoonish archetype of an American billionaire. He was a ventriloquist for all the people who looked upon Ivy Leaguers as snobbish elites, an alchemist harnessing the fear of immigrants that was also at the heart of the American story. He was the self-proclaimed savior of white men and women who felt like they had been left behind. Truth be told, I could sympathize with people who felt unrepresented, alienated, and excluded—even though I knew their solution was to get rid of me.

When Trump won, the shock was to feel personal. Everyone at Yale was stunned, as though the unthinkable had happened. We were all convinced he was an illiterate comedian—but really, the joke was on us. His victory would unleash all the ugly phantoms of America and the West, and throughout Europe, tyrants and nationalists would pop up, stoking revulsion toward immigrants and minorities. If one part of the legacy of the West was the Enlightenment, here was the other—white supremacy and fascism put into practice. Fascism was not just in the recent past of the West; it was practically tradition.

A moment of history was ending; a new moment was beginning—a new generation coming up. And between the death of the ancien régime and the birth of a new order, there would be a countermovement of hatred and violence, and a long night of desolation and chaos. Every institution would come under scrutiny, every structure challenged, every assumption questioned. Obama had cracked open the entire premise of white supremacy, but the inheritors of that tradition would not go away quietly.

I walked all over New York as dusk approached. I spent time alone in Central Park, and for a moment felt a gentle peace pass through me, a healing force that connected me to the work of generations before me. That work—of building a more generous, hopeful, liberated world—would continue, had to continue, but not without a fight. The fight was just starting, and I was preparing my mind for battle.

The subway beckoned. I boarded and was soon rattling through the New York underground, firing through Manhattan Island, through the American inferno, tumbling forward, northward, toward the refuge of Harlem.

24.

Good Trouble

In the spring of 2017, I graduated from Yale Law School. Donald Trump had been inaugurated that year and the pallor took over America.

My parents drove down to New Haven for the ceremony. Dada had battled chemotherapy but was looking fresh on this day. My brothers came down as well. Ali was in undergrad and had a crisp fade and was producing music; he was rebelling the way I once did and showed more interest in Dr. Dre than Descartes. Oz was working in finance and being a responsible young man, just as he had once been a responsible boy. We didn't speak that often, but had grown close in recent years.

I was more nervous about the reception the evening before than the actual ceremony. How would my parents behave among the other parents who were lawyers and hedge fund managers? How would they conduct themselves in this rich world that had conditioned me to hide and perform? The reception was in the beautiful Yale Law School courtyard. Other parents were around. Dada stood proudly in his baggy suit, Amma in her bright shalwar kameez and hijab. My grandmother couldn't attend. I remembered the feelings of shame I had when my mother would drop me at school, worried that other kids would see her clothes or hear her accent. My parents socialized with the other parents, Dada discussing his latest paint job, Amma speaking about her teacher days.

Dada, in particular, was happy to be among so many Jews. He always used to say that if a Jewish person was your doctor or your dentist, you never had to worry. In one absurd encounter, he sat next to a prominent Bush administration cabinet member and returned to tell me all about it.

"I sat with Michael Chertoff," Dada said cheerfully. "He was Bush's secretary of homeland security after 9/11. Man, oh man. He asked where I was from and I didn't want to lie so I told him I was born in Peshawar."

I observed my parents mingling. They were shy and reserved, and I thought of the long road they, and we, had traveled to get here. And what happened next left me unsettled.

The parents who evoked shame in my parents were, ironically, or maybe obviously, Pakistani. I nervously watched as my mother and father shook hands with the parents of a Pakistani classmate of mine. My classmate was from a well-heeled family, the sort to send their kids to private schools and on to Harvard and Yale for college. My friend's father was standing tall in a dark green suit, some sort of conglomerate owner who likely had enough wealth to purchase whole swaths of Lahore or Karachi. My friend's mother was decked out in a beautiful gold-embossed shalwar kameez.

Two sets of Pakistani parents, from two wildly different social classes, came together. I stood and watched. The parents said their "Salaams" in Urdu and then . . . nothing. The conversation went dead. They looked at each other, no words forthcoming. It was as though an impenetrable barrier had come between them, for in Pakistan people with such divergent backgrounds would never have interacted.

I thought of saying something to break the awkward silence, but I was too stunned to speak.

My friend's father glanced around for something to comment on. He looked at me and I looked back, but I would not engage in the performance. The seconds dragged on. All four were from the same country, yet could not talk to one another. Pakistanis—and Indians—could be the most classist of all people, condemning those without wealth or university education as somehow undeserving. So much for Islam making all people equal.

I looked to my father. He was searching for words. I knew he was ashamed of his own origins in the face of the conglomerate owner. After all, my father had never completed his university studies. My friend's father came from Pakistan's elite and he was surprised into silent tension that he was encountering a lower-class countryman in the courtyard of Yale Law School.

Dada mumbled something and wandered away to the buffet table—much as I had walked away from snobbish interactions at parties. How many times I had been in Dada's position, feeling out of place, choked for words, watching the stares of men believing themselves superior. American etiquette required us to feign equality here, but Pakistani class assumptions meant that two men with brown skin and the same language could not say a single word to each other.

I could feel the shame burning in my parents, felt the same shame within me. They were getting a glimpse of the worlds I had navigated and how isolated it had made me. My mother hovered close to me. Rarified spaces could constrict us, warp us, distort us so that our insides screamed for recognition. I thought of the words of James Baldwin: "The place in which I'll fit will not exist until I make it."

No matter how uncomfortable I became, I would persist in my existence and carve out my own place, make my own lane. I was proud to be graduating from Yale Law School, getting here through a circuitous, booby-trapped road from Scartown, but in that moment, I was proudest to be my parents' son.

• • •

The official ceremony was held the next day. Rain clapped down like shells from the sky. Dark clouds were gathering. I felt a distinct sadness within me. Despite having my family there for the ceremony, and having personally accomplished something of note, I was sad for the world around me. America, a great country, had been handed over to a corrupt autocrat. I felt like I had been conned in some way. The values I had been taught to live by had gotten me to this graduation stage, but the very first act of the new administration was to ban people who looked like me from America. My heart was broken. I felt like the vision of America I had believed in so long had been vandalized, like a dream had ended, and with it, the ideals of youth. It was as though I had recognized that day, wearing my graduation robes, that the very system that had trained me could, the very next moment, demand to see my papers and consider me a threat. The same system could do violence to my body—to other bodies who didn't graduate from

Yale, bodies that stood behind me at the airport after I showed my blue passport.

When the dean called my name, and I walked to shake his hand, I reflected on how poorly I had done in school as a child, how I felt misunderstood, like the world had preordained me a failure. I thought of the quiet nights alone, the days of being bullied, the friends I had lost. I had achieved a new life, yes, but the world had changed with me and demanded more action.

My friends crossed the stage. I heard the rain beating down outside. Then there was a pause in the auditorium. Heads turned to the entrance. And audible gasps could be heard as a small Black man approached the podium.

I knew who he was by face alone: Congressman John Lewis, the living legend, the liberator who had been beaten, battered, and bruised in his fight to realize America's ideals. He had been arrested forty times. He had been spat on, had cigarettes put out on him. Yet Lewis had persisted with love and nonviolence—studying Gandhi's method of satyagraha, the spiritual force of truth to fight back against hatred and bigotry.

Lewis was ailing now, three years away from his death, but the moment he touched the microphone it was like he transformed into a thirty-year-old Baptist preacher from Alabama.

"When we would visit the little town of Troy," Lewis said, his voice rising, "visit Tuskegee, visit Montgomery, and as a student in Nashville and later as someone living in Atlanta, I saw those signs that said 'White Men,' 'Colored Men'; 'White Women,' 'Colored Women'; 'White Waiting,' 'Colored Waiting.' Growing up, I would ask my mother, my father, my grandparents, my great-grandparents,

'Why?' They would say, 'That's the way it is. Don't get in the way. Don't get in trouble.' But in 1955, fifteen years old, in the tenth grade, I heard about Rosa Parks. I heard the words of Martin Luther King Jr. on our radio. The action of Rosa Parks and the words of Martin Luther King Jr. inspired me to *find a way to get in the way.* I got in the way. *I got in trouble.* Good trouble. Necessary trouble."

Lewis's voice echoed on. "My philosophy is very simple. When you see something that is not right, not fair, not just, you have a moral obligation to say something or do something."

If a voice could carry in its timbre the echoes of emancipation, then John Lewis's voice sung to the angels. There was a fierce urgency in his tone. Lewis was passing the torch to the next generation, our generation. I felt the distress lifting from my chest. We could not fall into misery or despair. We had to endure. Previous generations had not suffered for us to throw up our hands in defeat.

And I, too, was an inheritor of John Lewis's work. Like every brown-skinned person, I owed a debt to the Black Americans whose emancipation presaged the liberation of us all: Black, Asian, Indigenous, Brown, and yes, white people, too, who had the most work to do to become free. Darker days might be ahead, but I would not succumb to fear. I would try to serve the legacies of those who had made room for me and, crucially, those who were coming next.

The rain fell. I saw the scarred lines on Lewis's face. I saw the hopeful glances in my parents' eyes. And I felt hope.

• • •

Later that year, I returned to Canada. Trump being in office narrowed my prospects in the United States. Feeling no room to breathe, I wanted to give back to the nation that had made my education possible. Canada had invested in public schools, public health care, public scholarships, and a safety net for those who fell on hard times. These programs had been won with great difficulty and were directly linked to why I was able to go to university. My family never lived in fear of losing our health insurance. The public schools in my neighborhood had problems, but the teachers did their best. Though Canada had its own violent past, especially with respect to Indigenous peoples, there was still hope that progress could be made. Now it was time to give back.

That summer, I began working as a foreign policy advisor in Prime Minister Justin Trudeau's government. I was inspired by Trudeau's victory: a progressive leader who ushered in a new generation of leaders in Canada, soon to be envied around the world.

My role in government focused on human rights, Asia-Pacific issues—including China and North Korea—and international law. I worked out of the Foreign Ministry, directly for Chrystia Freeland, then the foreign minister. She was a brilliant former journalist—and brought a hardscrabble spirit to the job. Canada's sleepy government was finally waking up to the transformative realities of the twenty-first century. The Department of Foreign Affairs looked like a brown Aztec temple, and I was soon shuttling between there and the Prime Minister's Office, which looked like a grand estate. Parliament Hill resembled the House of Commons in Britain, but bigger. There was a lake around the buildings and another stone edifice across the street where the prime minister worked.

Those first weeks were consumed by phone calls, briefings, meetings at the Prime Minister's Office, and big policy ideas at the

Foreign Office. A phone call had to be arranged between the foreign minister and the head of the Burmese military who was carrying out an ethnic cleansing of Rohingya Muslims. What message would we convey? What would be the strategy? How would we coordinate across departments? What was Washington saying? I made the argument that we had to use the strongest language possible—call it a genocide and demand an international inquiry. In the evening, I would dial in and take notes in a phone call with the US secretary of state or the British foreign secretary. From what I heard, Trump and Trudeau had a warm personal relationship. Trump even took a liking to Trudeau, probably because when Trump looked at Trudeau, the president saw a younger version of himself. Good looks and money were all that mattered in his world.

One day early on, I was called to the PMO for an urgent meeting. It was like something out of *The West Wing*—walking into a highly secure briefing room. The situation was dire. A Canadian pastor had been imprisoned in North Korea for two years after trying to deliver humanitarian aid. A message had come through diplomatic channels at the United Nations in New York that North Korea wanted to talk. The implication was that our pastor was severely ill and Kim Jong-un wanted to bargain. The question before us was whether Justin Trudeau should dispatch a special envoy to North Korea.

Normally, there would have been no problem in meeting secretly—these kinds of meetings happened all the time, even though Canada and North Korea did not have diplomatic relations. What made this unique was the time frame: President Donald J. Trump had tweeted "Fire and Fury" that week and Kim had called

America's president a "frightened dog" and "a mentally challenged dotard." It was like the Cuban Missile Crisis all over again, but with children in charge.

So I was sitting in the room, listening to all this, when a stern-looking blond woman turned to me and said, "You're the policy advisor, right? What's your recommendation?"

This was not a drill. No matter how much I had prepared, nothing could capture the visceral realness of being in the room and called upon. Perhaps this was a realization every generation had eventually: that we were in charge now.

I delivered my opinion. I left the room with ice in my veins. Trudeau would send the envoy, taking a huge risk, as nuclear war hung in the balance that week. All I could think of was how Steve Bannon still worked in the White House and had disturbing neo-Crusader-white-supremacist-end-of-times ideas. Or the legal fact that all executive authority in the United States was vested in a single individual: the president. It was startling to see just how much of war and peace was dependent on the psyche of a few men.

We received word through back channels from President Trump's national security advisor, General H. R. McMaster, who said that the US expressed no dissent for the secret mission to North Korea. He also said that we could deliver a message to the North Korean leadership: the United States did not seek regime change in Pyong-yang. This was another huge relief because McMaster's boss was declaring on Twitter that America was "Locked and Loaded."

In my room that weekend, I read *The Best and the Brightest*, the 1972 book by the late *Washington Post* reporter David Halberstam. The author had chronicled the brain trust of the Kennedy administration, the liberal intellectuals, scholars, bankers, lawyers, and military men who arrived in Washington in 1960, many of them from Harvard and Yale. This was the story of how the brightest minds in America, full of hubris and arrogance, led the country into the worst foreign policy decision of the twentieth century with the Vietnam War. Yet the title—*The Best and the Brightest*—became a kind of shorthand for upward mobility. People often ignored that the title of the book was meant to be ironic: it was often the smartest, most credentialed, most confidently opinionated people who, with power in their hands, made the most foolish decisions. And I was a member of that tribe. Sometimes I wondered if it wasn't our very polished letters, our glittering words, our well-heeled educations, that made us blind.

A day later, I got the note that the pastor and the envoy were departing Pyongyang. Trump had not blown up the entire operation at the last minute. The world did not end. I exhaled and went back to the office, where another crisis was waiting for me.

$\cdots$

Government is a slow, monstrous beast. Legislation takes time to pass. Political leaders are always susceptible to public opinion and pressure. International relations are further complicated by the fact that personal relationships between leaders or foreign ministers do not change much. What matters to any government are its national (or partisan) interests: realpolitik, the reality of politics.

But government is also meant to be representative. So what happens when the people in charge don't look like you or the neighborhoods that produced you? Western governments, including Canada's, had been created by white men to serve white men. They had enforced colonial laws, punished the darker-skinned, and killed off whole groups. The residues of that racism were still present.

Before I started my job, I got a phone call from a senior person who said, "Observe the people in the room and be careful who you talk to." *Strange*, I thought, and like every other time I've been warned about something, I thought it would not apply to me.

The incidents began as small occurrences. A white man who cut me off during a meeting before I could finish my argument. A white man who said, in a room full of people, "Don't tell us what we already know"—even though it was evident he didn't know the subject at hand. I would say hello to another white person who had an office near mine, but they treated me like I was a piece of furniture. I counted one minority and one woman in meetings with twenty people. I viewed these as the necessary turf wars of government, steeled my skin, and always kept a smile on my face.

Despite being given many of the "brown files" that were at the bottom of the heap, I dove joyfully into them. I loved the actual *work* of public service: the policy meetings no one would ever hear about, helping a constituent solve an issue raised to our office, thinking always how the government could advance human rights, coordinating with other offices on a major policy announcement that had been worked on for months. But things began to worsen—in petty and unfortunate ways, the sort of thing that might seem minor now, but was hugely consequential every day. I was left off email chains that involved my files—an indirect form of sabotage. I was given misinformation about the location or time of a meeting, which left me scrambling at the last moment to avoid disaster. A white person proceeded to explain the history of India to me as though I had never heard of that country. Old white bureaucrats, men, would talk over me, lecture about why an original policy idea was dead on arrival. Their world was stuck in the 1950s, but the world outside our windows had changed. When I was sitting in front of them, I sometimes wondered if they even realized how out of touch they sounded. We were headed directly for disaster on so many issues—climate change, China, India, Russia, nuclear proliferation, cybercrime, extreme inequality, the fate of democracy—yet this old guard acted as though nothing urgent was on the line. The status quo had served them, but I was there to disrupt their certitudes.

Gradually, I was being excluded, ignored, and silenced, my sense of worth invalidated. What was worse: the people in charge had no clue about the subtle discrimination taking place around us. Usually, I was the only minority in any meeting: a sea of white faces and me, holding my own, representing, and doing my best not to come off as "aggressive," "too articulate," or "uppity." I knew that some white people feared people of color who could talk to them as equals. I made myself smaller to not bruise their egos and rarely called out behavior that was beginning to take a toll on my mental health. I questioned my own reality: Was I being too impatient? Unkind? Moving too fast? Too arrogant? Too sensitive? Afflicted with best-and-brightest syndrome? My emotions swung wildly from frustration to defensiveness to exhaustion to forgiveness. I made excuses for my colleagues' remarks and attitudes. They were busy people. They had a lot on their hands. I used my lawyer jujitsu to convince myself that *I* was the problem. So what if they can't see me? This is how things are. Don't get in the way.

I began to write memos on what I was witnessing. I wrote memos on how to improve our policy-making process, enhance our coordination, and create a conveyor belt from policy creation to completion to communication. I wrote briefing notes and memos that went nowhere.

One day that fall, I was invited to a BBQ in a senior official's backyard. Almost every invited guest was white. There were emissaries and important people there. A woman handed me a garbage bag when I arrived. She expected me to know what to do. I was confused for a second because she knew who I was. Then I understood. And instead of speaking up, doing something, saying, "I am not here to clean up your trash, I work for the prime minister," I just took the bag, walked around the party, and collected everyone's garbage. They were happy to give it to me. My throat constricted in shame and disgust. For the entire party, I didn't say a word to anyone. I cleaned up their dishes, wiped their spilled drinks, took their litter. In fact, I was so angry that I cleaned up after them with *extra* dedication. I hated myself for obliging and hated the fact that I was at their mercy. I wondered what my parents and grandmother would say if they saw me. They, too, had been treated as colonial subjects, as had my ancestors. And these white people? They were enacting the roles they expected of themselves and of me, and any challenge to their authority would have been met with anger. Why could I not speak up? I was powerless in their system. For three hours I walked around with that bag, then drove home in silence.

When I visited my parents and Amma asked me what was

wrong, I snapped at her. "Leave me alone." I was constantly irritable and anxious—and on the worst days, felt hopelessly suffocating.

This was the unvarnished truth of the system from the inside. Systemic racism infected the structure of every operation and filtered down to the individuals in the organization. Justin Trudeau was not the person I blamed: there was a culture of exclusion at the top echelons of government. That culture had taught certain white people that covert discrimination was acceptable. This was true of all the power centers in the West, which would be the last to let go of old habits. These institutions, after all, were not made with the colored person in mind. They were meant to subject us and control us.

We often speak of racism as though it is a purely emotional phenomenon, but racism manifests itself in the body, and the body responds to it like a disease. Cortisol levels spike, increasing the chance of every possible illness. Your heartbeat quickens. Your limbs go tense. There is a psychological cost of staying ahead. You doubt your own abilities. You question your own self-worth. A huge amount of mental energy goes into anticipating and responding to other people's slights. You try to speak—but now have been silenced from within. And for individuals who come from disadvantaged backgrounds and work their way up—always having to be twice as good—research shows that their *cells age faster* because of the accumulated stresses. Their lives are literally being cut short because of racism.

Nor is this only about the individual. Discrimination at the micro level destabilizes any team's greatest resource: its talent. At the macro level, the whole organization underperforms because crucial signals that minorities can deliver are neglected. At the end of the day, racism is not only a benighted mindset. It is simply bad for business.

For me, the trouble with seeing the game from the inside was bearing witness to the fact that we had such a long way to go. A generation's worth of work to decolonize our minds and learn, for the first time, what it means to treat others with respect. The system as it existed was still reproducing injustices—for society, and for the people working within it. This same system had educated me, reared me, nearly owned me—and so when I made any mention of racism, I was also fighting a war within myself: suppress it, ignore it, censor it, surpass it, transcend it, deny it. At last, I chose to accept it. I knew my own faults, too, being impatient with the status quo and arguing for big changes. But if not now, when? If not this generation, which one? Not every person felt they had the luxurious patience for moderation.

When I realized I could not make any change from within, I decided to resign with my dignity intact. I wanted to get into trouble, necessary trouble. I had come too far to be just another native informant happy to be here, grateful for the establishment's patronage, excited to be a pleasant token.

I was not here to fit in anymore. I was here to make room.

. . .

Shortly before I resigned, I arrived at Parliament Hill in a dark blue suit, with a binder under my arm. I was bleary-eyed from a long flight. The meeting was held over Burma, the continued ethnic cleansing of the Rohingya Muslims.

After the other advisors had left, I hung back at the office. It was just me and Justin Trudeau in the room—an extreme rarity, since Trudeau always had handlers nearby.

The prime minister had a cold that day and was blowing his nose behind his desk, head turned away. He didn't realize I was standing there. Up close, Trudeau was even more striking than in photos—his long face and bright eyes radiated warmth and goodwill. I knew how ruthless he was internally, and that Trudeau's closest advisors held tightly the levers of power. Trudeau, son of power, knew how power had to be used. He knew just how fragile the progressive project had become, with populist conservatives winning across the Western world. But he was also a victim of his own good intentions.

On the wall there was a photo of his father, Pierre Elliott Trudeau, carrying little Justin. That was the man responsible for my own father's journey to Canada—for opening a white country to Brown and Asian immigrants.

"Prime Minister," I said.

Trudeau looked up, startled to see me standing there.

I began to speak, to tell him who I was, but he already knew. The prime minister came around to the table and put his hand on my arm, nodding.

I said, "I want you to know that my father was a great admirer of your father, and it's because of Pierre Elliott Trudeau that my dad could come to Canada."

Trudeau gave his familiar smile.

I thought of whether to tell him about what I witnessed around me. I wondered whether Trudeau was the real deal or if this was all a performance for him—like it was for so many people who were born into privilege and became politicians. His heart did seem to be in the right place, and Trudeau genuinely seemed to care for the future of his country, and the planet. With Prime Minister Trudeau right in front of me, and his father's picture behind him, I imagined my own father's journey to Canada, the long lines, the cold weather. He would have been just another file in some bureaucratic office—a number to be accepted or rejected. Had the bureaucrat reviewing his application been sick that day, or fought with his wife the night before, he might well have denied Dada immigration.

In an instant, generations were transcended, a loop closed from 1971, the year Dada arrived in Canada, to 2017. We were two very different men, having traveled two very different paths, as had our fathers. Yet here we were. It was strange and unpredictable how time unfolded, a reminder that the work of democracy was ultimately unfinished—and about serving those not yet born. What kind of world would we leave to them? What kind of planet?

Trudeau said a few words. We talked a little more. Then I apologetically said goodbye, leaving his office for the last time.

When I turned, I saw a troubled man in profile, alone with his thoughts, the door closing, the prime minister tending to his runny nose.

25.

Inheritance

For two years, I wandered. I went from one New England town to another, living in cabins, surviving on the goodwill of others, alone in the woods. After running for so long, I had finally come to a stop. It was the somber solitude of the forest, the quiet winters in upstate New York and New Hampshire, the nightly shivers of the trees, that began to relieve some of the darkness in my heart. I had pushed down the pain of the slights and rejections and family dysfunctions and racial judgments for so long that, for a couple of years, I just disappeared.

The phone calls came at first, and then my phone stopped ringing entirely. I hibernated for three winters and summers. In my cabin, I pulled together the threads that I had never understood, letting the memories settle before they rushed out in a flood. Memory was testimony, a record of partial truths, a reclamation of personal history. Memory was imperfect, but it was a record that could be preserved, a way of seeing. I was trying to expunge the harshest memories, to heal myself from any resentments or grudges. I thought of the white people I had met, those I was fond of, those who had belittled me, and I kept their grimaces and grins away from my heart, not wishing to feel those emotions again.

I wanted to forgive, to be forgiven. I thought of what Sartre had said, that freedom was what you did with what's been done to you. Education had been my liberation, had taught me to construct in my skull a working mind, but had also transformed me to the point that I sometimes cracked under the weight of my own multiplicities. "I am large," wrote Whitman, "I contain multitudes." Sometimes, behind my eyelids, I felt a multitude of emptiness.

There, among my books, and the dark rustling trees, I saw my folder of identities: a college diploma, a master's degree, a law degree, résumés, letters of introduction. So glittering they looked, these gold badges I had chased for merit—and for whom? Did I not just risk becoming another well-credentialed brown face in a white empire? It occurred to me that at every step of the way, there was someone—some force, some face—telling me that I was no good and had to keep getting the blessings of a system that was never made for me in the first place. This was what it all amounted to, a big white voice and a tiny dark echo in my ears that said: *Keep this Brown boy running.* I stared at those documents, those identities— and now I thought of burning them all. I recognized that my real education, and real knowledge, could not be contained in a piece of paper in a dead language I could not even read.

The seasons changed; I changed. There was a time I craved the validation those papers symbolized; now I knew that true authority came from within. But these gold stickers were part of a journey, and they had taught me that no matter where we came from or how we looked or what we believed, even in an unjust society, we could hunger for more: more community, more love, more learning, more questions, more freedom, more life.

For over a decade, I had been trying to find home. I had traveled and read and fought and found my identity shattered and re-created. I had sought a home in the idealized future, in the unromanticized past, a past that could not be outrun. And though I tried to construct a sturdy home within my own heart, I was missing one essential piece of the story. The thought began to gnaw at me, slowly at first, then at all hours.

The snow fell, blockading me by the fireplace. Only the hills and trees were around me. A black pen, a notepad. Early in the morning, I saw the sun rising behind the mountain: a dark, triangular silhouette with glowing lines, like it was drawn by God. The sun warmed my eyes, and I began to prepare to end this withdrawal into the wilderness.

I could feel my inheritances rushing forth, warning me of a final trial, whispering a prayer, voices from the past—the dead and undead—encouraging me to reemerge once again, to pull myself out of this hole and come back home.

· · ·

But first—the clock stopped for a year and a half.

I returned home in March 2020, expecting to stay two weeks, and ended up at last spending quality time with my parents. I stayed in the room where my grandmother had stayed for fifteen years—Dadiye had been moved to a nursing home just before the pandemic. As we sheltered in place, in the darkness and spring and summer, I would hear the sounds of coughing from my father's room, heard my mother praying in another room, her forehead touching the mat, with a cat on either side. I spent my time teaching others, helping students with their writing, giving away all the lessons I had learned to any youngster who would listen. I helped my father where I could, helped lighten the burden my mother had carried on her shoulders for sixty years.

The last thing I did before the world, and life, came to a frightening standstill, I was visiting Dadiye in the nursing home. It felt eerie to be there, around the elderly struggling for comfort, but Dadiye had her same strong face and soft hands and head full of long white hair: the matriarch, my grandmother. She had a Qur'an open by her nursing home bed, and looked as though she had been waiting for me for hours.

"*Hein?*" she said, looking up. "You have returned, *beta*, come, come." Dadiye apologized for not being able to offer me tea. I hugged her and told her it was fine.

She was almost ninety now, had seen two-thirds of the twentieth century, had witnessed, as a girl, a teenager, a woman, a wife, a mother, a grandmother, a great-grandmother the wreckage and continuous rebuilding of the world.

Suddenly, Dadiye's eyes narrowed. She looked at me sternly, lovingly, and loudly said, "Why haven't you gotten married! Tomorrow! Tomorrow! We will marry you off tomorrow!"

I laughed. I gave her the bouquet of flowers. I wished her a happy birthday. And I told her I would come and sit with her longer, read my books and do my work next to her right from the nursing home. She said she would wait, just like my mother and father had waited, waited for me to call, waited for my brothers to come home, waited for me to say I love you even when I didn't have the words, waited for me to grow older, waited, waited.

I told Dadiye I would come back and ask her more questions. It was the only untruth I ever told her.

• • •

On Thanksgiving Day, Dadiye passed away from COVID-19, taking her final breath through a video call screen. This woman who had helped raise me had said her final prayers. Taken by the virus in a hospital room.

I did visit Dadiye in the hospital two days before, but she had been unconscious, an oxygen mask on her face. And I whispered, "Wake up, Dadiye." And I whispered, "I'm here." And I whispered, "I love you," and I touched her leg—but no words were spoken back. It was as though we had, in the end, simply run out of time.

There would never be another conversation, another hug. Amma recited the prayer to be said at the dying person's final moment. My father could not bear to look.

I felt an overwhelming grief that was punctured only when Amma said, in Urdu, "*Khuda Hafiz. Acha vaqt ghuzra.*" Goodbye. We had a wonderful time.

Two days later, Dadiye was laid to rest on the outskirts of Toronto, where she had served her duty as a mother and grandmother. After a long, fitful life, she had earned her rest. It was a cold, overcast day. Only ten people were allowed to attend, and in the end, only nine came. Iqbal Mian, who had in fact been Dadiye's younger son, did not even show up. Some grudges from bygone eras would be taken to the grave. The silence that creaked between the nine family members—my parents, my brothers, my uncle and cousin—stretched back the near-century of Dadiye's life. Those memories we shared would now become like private relics, stored deep in the senses, to be recalled in strange moments and other rooms, always with a pause or a smile.

As my grandmother was laid to rest, I felt an inexhaustible breath in my chest, inhale and exhale. There was no call to prayer for the *janaza*, the prayer before a Muslim was buried. That Azan had been delivered the day the dead was born, as a child, into their ears. So we came around full circle, from the womb's earth and into the earth's womb—and so I sank into an impenetrable darkness of heartbreak and grief. I could hardly get myself up from the bed, the ghosts of "Get scholarship" and my grandmother's walks with me and Oz to Parkway Mall when we were kids replaying in my head, along with the stories she had shared with me about the past.

I would close my eyes and it was as though I was a little boy again in that bungalow in Scartown, running between Dadiye and Amma as the snow fell outside, lost in my imagination, bounded by a world of love that was much older than me.

Other stories soon came to light. My grandmother's late older brother, the doctor from London, the mustached man whose photo was in our house—had served in the British Indian Army in World War II. He had taken shrapnel to the head during the liberation of Italy, from the weapons not of an Italian fascist, but of the Nazis. The shrapnel remained lodged in his skull his entire life, the doctor figuring it was too dangerous to operate even after he was back in peacetime London. All of Dadiye's older brothers had fought valiantly in the Second World War, defeating fascism and Nazism for the empire that had made them subjects. I learned, despite my heartbreak and sadness, that my forefathers were part of that great colonized generation who, denied their own freedoms, still fought and died for the freedom of the entire world.

• • •

After Dadiye's death, the Toronto suburbs were haunted for me. The loss of my grandmother drove me into a deep and inconsolable depression. Heartbreak and the pandemic thrown on top left my brain paralyzed. I was tortured by regrets, by thoughts of what I could have done to not be abandoned by love and hope. Time had stopped, and yet the pandemic had robbed us of so much time that everything was a blur.

For the first time, I understood how a human being could kill themselves. I smoked dozens of cigarettes a day to numb the pain. When I went on my walks, despite bundling up, I felt an ice-cold chill passing through me, through my tendons and lungs—the spirit of death, I thought of it later, the cousin of sleep, as the dead began to surround me, slipping away into eternal darkness, grandmothers and fathers and sisters, all passing away slowly, quietly, without a cry or howl.

Finally, after some months of being unable to sleep or eat or even think, I sought professional help.

My psychologist asked me over the phone: "Are you suicidal?"

I replied, somewhat annoyed: "Not in the literal sense, but I am killing myself slowly."

Nothing was able to shake off the decay I felt within me. I even prayed again, prayed late at night, begged to God, *Please help me.*

And as the winter turned to summer and the summer turned to fall, I grew a few more white hairs and had a few more aches in my hands—but finally, in my search for hope, I saw a sliver of light, a moment to depart, to go back full circle and find my own renewal.

That fall, I boarded a plane to Pakistan late at night. After twenty-eight years, I was making the fourteen-hour journey to my parents' homeland, the journey long-deferred, to the place where it all began.

. . .

One day in early October 2021, I arrived in Islamabad after a long flight during which I reread the history of Murree and Pakistan and India. I was going to an old colonial town up in the mountains, to the place where my mother and all my grandfathers and grandmothers on Amma's side of the family had been raised—a place that Dadiye was said to have adored.

I stepped out into a humid evening, and my auntee was there to greet me. She waved me down and I followed her to the car.

"Come on, son," she said. "This is my nephew."

I said "Salaam" to the curly-mustached young man driving the car. We roared down the speedway and it felt like I was tasting air for the first time—hot air, gulps of it, in the very country where my parents had come from.

"So," said the young man driving. "Your name is Omer. This is a beautiful name, you know."

We came to a stop. Three or four colorfully dressed people walked up to different cars asking for money. Several cars drove right through the red light as if it weren't there. A motorcycle with three men, all wearing shalwar kameez, ripped ahead and left a cloud of smoke around us.

The young driver next to me said, "If one car stop, we all stop. If first car go, we all go. This is Pakistan."

As we drove, I considered his earlier comment. Never had someone told me my name was beautiful or special. Not in Toronto or Paris or New York. My name in the West had been associated with menacing faces. For the first time in my life, I fully inhabited this name of mine with pride.

We drove until we got to Rawalpindi, the garrison town where the armed forces were headquartered. It was a calm, cool evening in Pakistan; the clouds were gathering to pour out the late monsoon rains. The whiff of spices and tobacco was in the air.

I brought my suitcase into the house and began to unpack my things, feeling the jet lag of the long journey. I felt like I had touched down where I was meant to be, where I had to come for everything else to make sense. The darkness, the awakening, the lightness, the mind-expansion of education, the depression: it all lead back to the mountains of my kin and skin.

"Rest now," Auntee said. "Tomorrow we will go to your mother's village."

...

The roads leading to Murree were treacherous. The hills and mountains were seven thousand feet above the ground, the range of snowy peaks that open up to the land of Kashmir. As we drove in a winding circle up toward the heavens, we left the city far behind. The air cooled. The bustle of the country died down so that the only sounds were the purring motor of the car and the flick of a lighter to spark a cigarette.

I looked out the window at the tallest trees I had seen in my life, a clear blue sky, cliffs that fell hundreds of feet, and glorious green hills that dotted the distance—and I felt a twist of panic.

The car swerved past potholes, and my cousin, who was driving, recounted tales from the past, the exploits of an uncle, the wedding of an auntee, the paving of this new road up the hills. Pakistan, I was to learn very quickly, was a nation of storytellers, and nearly every conversation I had led back to a parable, a myth, or folklore from the mountains. With each story I heard, I was thrown back into another kind of history, an oral history that had been otherwise unknown to me, and I began to feel a kinship with this past that I was slowly recovering, in fragments. My history had for so long been written by and for others; in returning to Murree, in meeting my relatives and listening to their stories, I was reclaiming some pieces of history all for myself.

"See how the winds have picked up?" my cousin said, puffing on a cigarette. "It wasn't like this always. The weather has gotten worse, much worse. Climate change." He inhaled deeply, and the smoke rushed out of his nose. "Something terrible is coming from above, *bhai*."

It was explained to me by my uncles and auntees that our maternal ancestors were from this village. Amma was born here; her parents were born in Murree; their parents were born and raised here. The Abbassi clan was said to have taken its name from the Abbasid Caliphate that once ruled Baghdad. They had become farmers and construction workers in the hills of British India, and Murree became a summer holiday retreat for the viceroys and administrators of the empire. On the drive, I saw the schools and churches named after Christian luminaries. There was even a rumor—known to the locals—that the name Murree was taken from the Virgin Mary, who was believed to be buried at Pindi Point up in the hills. Another legend in this place of myths was that the Abbassid caliph, Harun al-Rashid, from *One Thousand and One Nights*, had sent the first Abbassi family members to the Indian subcontinent. Somehow, when my eyes were wide open, I always discovered a new story. The family had lived together, created a world of their own in the mountains, had made themselves anew—a tribe of doers and makers who carried the sturdy resolve of a people from the mountains. Theirs was a simple world of faith and diligence. Soon, I would learn that all the women on my mother's side of the family, who lived in Murree, were teachers. Amma had been a teacher, too, and some of her students were now grown women, with kids of their own, studying in the same schools—Lawrence College, Covenant of Jesus and Mary—that were revered in Murree.

The car slowed to a crawl. We pulled onto a dirt road. The sun was setting behind the hills, giving off a light blue mist that covered the horizon.

I walked slowly toward the little house. It had a corrugated iron roof, broken stones, earthen walls. A small gate, a humble courtyard. I was standing in front of the little house in the village of my past where my mother had been raised. The house where my parents had been married.

Little children stopped their playtime to come see me. Kids

from around Murree had heard the news and were running toward the house as their parents walked behind them, old mothers and grandfathers coming to see the son of the West who had at last come home.

Murree, I thought. *This village. From this village of Murree to Scartown and Paris and Yale Law School. From the mud hut to the Ivy League.* It was a preposterous thought—except it was true. And I felt an overwhelming gratitude for the life I had been given, for the strength I had been handed, able-bodied, strong-armed, brown-skinned, and the life I had molded. The canvas given to me from before my birth had already been beautiful; all I had done was freely paint my own strokes.

The world was a deep blue around me, oceanic, as evening fell. It was like being under water and above the clouds at the same time. I quietly followed my auntee to the gate of the cemetery next to the house. She whispered to me and pointed out two gray stones. "That is where your grandparents are buried."

An elderly man watched me, watched from the side of the mosque next to the land of graves, with a gaze that asked, *What took you so long?*

The kids from the village gathered near me. Some looked as young as three or four, and I recognized then that the last time I was in Murree, I had been their age.

I walked among the quiet dead until I came to two small headstones. My grandparents were buried here, as were their grandparents, and their grandparents, in unadorned graves in this small cemetery.

The lights flickered on across the hills like fireflies. From the loudspeaker, the Azan, the call to prayer, rang out. A soft voice echoed the words in Arabic.

I stopped before the headstones of my ancestors, and in that moment of immense grief, I felt the soil of my blood under my feet, and the fact that this village had birthed me and made me, and that I had come back to the roots that had always been waiting for me. I fell to my knees in a silent prayer, to the heavens and the past, and I wept for the journey that began in this village. I felt the love of two parents who had undertaken long migrations to give me life, and the many people of every color who had lifted me up, and Amma for her steady faith and Dada for his stern mind and, yes, God, too, who had cut me open only to let the light enter my inner frame. From this colonial town, this colonial history, I had emerged, and I had returned. There were no more masks or disguises now. There was no more running, no more hiding. Only the divine breath of these mountains around me and the ancestors above me and the little children watching beside me. The story would go on from here, as would I, passing on what I had learned, the knowledge and memories to be created and remade by the future, stories that would be revealed and rediscovered again.

Far above in the mountains, I found something sacred. And far away, beneath the dark rolling hills of the republic—

Unbetrayed by a lack of cynicism, I let life carry me down its river-stream—and I was free.

Acknowledgments

Sometimes, it really does take a village. Writing and publishing a book is an example of this *par excellence*. Writing—although solitary—requires institutions, families, friends, networks of support, and I was the beneficiary of all. Thanking everyone would be impossible, but a few words of appreciation are necessary.

I am grateful to my agent, Bonnie Nadell, who was a helpful sage through the publishing process, and to Valerie Steiker, who championed my early ideas. Thanks to all the good people at Scribner who believed in this project: Kathy Belden, an editorial genius, whose sharp eye and even sharper questions pushed me to think harder about the issues raised in this book; Rebekah Jett for her valued assistance; Nan Graham and the entire Scribner family. Thanks also to Jon Karp—now CEO of Simon & Schuster—for taking that meeting with a law student all those years ago.

The Canada Arts Council, Ontario Arts Council, and Toronto Arts Council were indispensable to the research and completion of this book. Residencies at MacDowell and Yaddo gave me the time and space to think about the layers of the story. The Logan Nonfiction Program allowed me to draft the earliest chapters. Lincoln Caplan at Yale Law School provoked me to think more about the

Acknowledgments

relationship between narrative and argument. Institutions are ultimately made up of people, and I would like to especially thank the administrative and service staffs of the residencies and fellowships I received, and the service and janitorial staffs of Yale Law School.

I am grateful to my parents, to my family, to my close friends, to the city of Toronto, and to the artists, musicians, writers, and painters who inspired me along the way. Without them, this book would not exist.

This is for the teachers—and for the students coming up next.

About the Author

Omer Aziz is a lawyer, writer, and former foreign policy advisor. He was born to working-class parents of Pakistani origin in Toronto, Canada, and became the first in his family to go to college in the West, later studying in Paris, at Cambridge, and at Yale Law School. He has clerked for the United Nations special envoy for Syria, served as a foreign policy advisor in the government of Canadian prime minister Justin Trudeau, and has written for the *New York Times*, the *Atlantic*, *New York Magazine*, the *New Republic*, and many other publications. He is currently a Radcliffe Fellow at Harvard University and lives in Cambridge, Massachusetts. *Brown Boy* is his first book.